M000267558

Contents

How to Use This Book

The centers in this book are designed to be completed in a small-group setting. All materials are included for groups of up to 6 students. The activities have been carefully crafted to meet the needs of students receiving Tier 2 Response to Intervention instruction, as well as the needs of any other students who are learning foundational phonics skills. The target skills in *Consonant Digraphs and Blends* include recognizing the sounds of frequently used digraphs and blends and applying those sounds to read words.

For the Teacher

Lesson Plan The skills in each unit are taught through teacher-led explicit instruction and are practiced through phonemic-awareness, hands-on, and written activities.

A fully scripted lesson plan cycles through auditory, oral, visual, and hands-on letter-sound activities that help students decode and read new words.

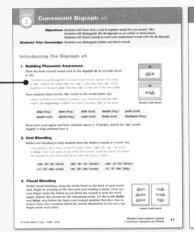

Scaffolded activities help guide students through the lesson.

front   *back*

Sound Cards

Vocabulary cards feature target sounds and aid students in blending sounds to read words.

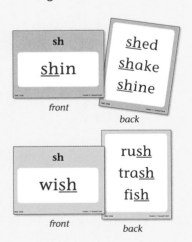

front   back

front   back

Answer Keys

Each center includes a two-sided page of answer keys, showing mat activities on one side and written application activities on the other side.

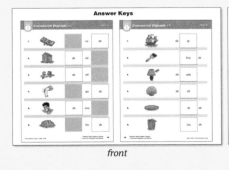

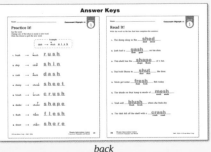

front   back

For the Student

Activity Mats and Task Cards

Each unit has six sets of activity mats and corresponding task cards, providing individual group members with their own materials for practicing the target skill.

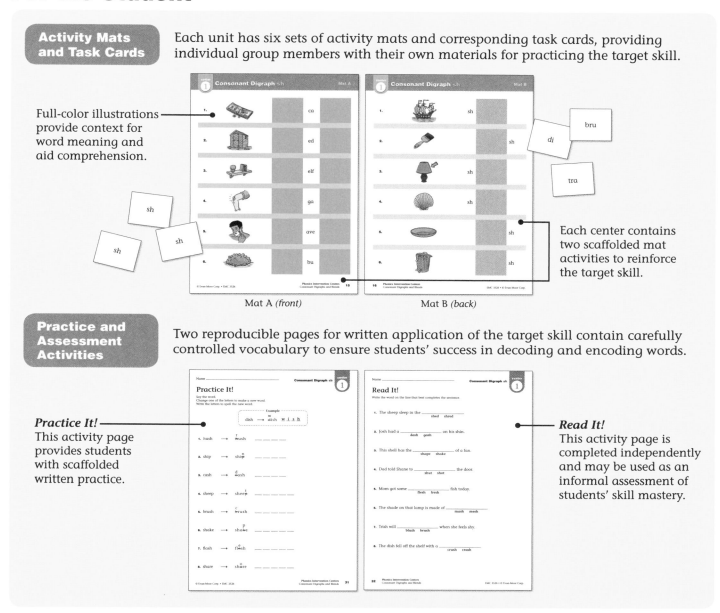

Full-color illustrations provide context for word meaning and aid comprehension.

Mat A *(front)*   Mat B *(back)*

Each center contains two scaffolded mat activities to reinforce the target skill.

Practice and Assessment Activities

Two reproducible pages for written application of the target skill contain carefully controlled vocabulary to ensure students' success in decoding and encoding words.

Practice It!
This activity page provides students with scaffolded written practice.

Read It!
This activity page is completed independently and may be used as an informal assessment of students' skill mastery.

Record Forms

Two reproducible record forms are included for tracking and assessing students' progress, individually or as a group. The *Group Progress Record* provides space for written comments and an assessment of skill mastery for each student in a particular group. The *Student Progress Record* includes a detailed breakdown of each center's objectives to informally assess an individual student's skill mastery.

How to Make and Store the Centers

You Will Need

- pocket-style folders (1 per center)
- business-size envelopes or small, self-locking plastic bags (12 per center)
- scissors, tape, marking pen
- laminating materials and equipment

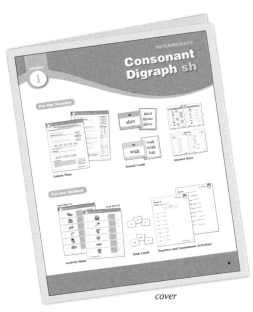

cover

Steps to Follow (for each center)

1. Remove the perforated pages and laminate all color pages. (Do not laminate the *Practice It!* and *Read It!* activities.)

2. Attach the cover page to the front of the folder.

3. Place the lesson plan in the left-hand pocket.

4. Cut apart the sound cards and the set of answer keys and place them with the lesson plan in the left-hand pocket of the folder.

5. Place all activity mats in the right-hand pocket.

6. Cut apart the task cards for Mat A and Mat B and sort them by student number (located on the back of most cards).

7. Keep each set of cards in a separate envelope or plastic bag and place them in the right-hand pocket of the folder.

8. Reproduce one copy of the *Practice It!* and *Read It!* activities for each student and place them in the right-hand pocket of the folder.

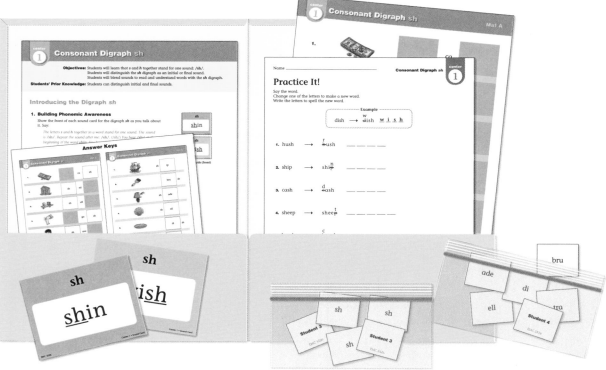

Phonics Intervention Centers
Consonant Digraphs and Blends

Group: _____

Date: _____

Group Progress Record

Center _____

Name	Comments	Assessment Level

Phonics Intervention Centers
Consonant Digraphs and Blends

Student Progress Record

Assessment Levels
M = mastered
N = needs more practice
R = reteach

	Date / Assessment	Date / Assessment	Date / Assessment
1 Consonant Digraph *sh*			
Recognizes that the *sh* digraph stands for the /sh/ sound			
Distinguishes the *sh* digraph as an initial or final sound			
Reads and understands words with the *sh* digraph			
2 Consonant Digraph *ch*			
Recognizes that the *ch* digraph stands for the /ch/ sound			
Distinguishes the *ch* digraph as an initial or final sound			
Reads and understands words with the *ch* digraph			
3 Consonant Digraph *th*			
Recognizes that the *th* digraph stands for the /th/ sound			
Distinguishes the *th* digraph as an initial or final sound			
Reads and understands words with the *th* digraph			
4 Consonant Digraphs Review			
Reads and understands words with the digraph *sh*, *ch*, or *th*			
5 Consonant + *r* Blends			
Recognizes the blends *br*, *cr*, *dr*, *fr*, *gr*, *pr*, and *tr*			
Blends individual sounds into words			
Reads and understands words with an initial *r* blend			
6 Consonant + *l* Blends			
Recognizes the blends *bl*, *cl*, *fl*, *gl*, *pl*, and *sl*			
Blends individual sounds into words			
Reads and understands words with an initial *l* blend			
7 Initial *s* Blends			
Recognizes the blends *sc*, *sk*, *sm*, *sn*, *sp*, *st*, and *sw*			
Blends individual sounds into words			
Reads and understands words with an initial *s* blend			
8 Consonant Blends Review			
Reads and understands words with an initial *r*, *l*, or *s* blend			

Consonant Digraph sh

For the Teacher

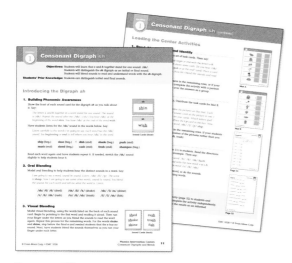

Lesson Plan

sh

shin

shed
shake
shine

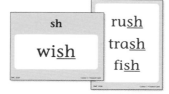

sh

wish

rush
trash
fish

Sound Cards

Answer Keys

Answer Keys

For the Student

front (Mat A)

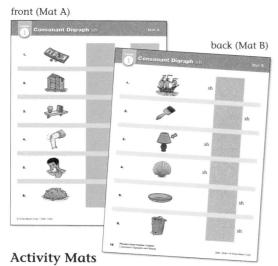

back (Mat B)

Activity Mats

Task Cards

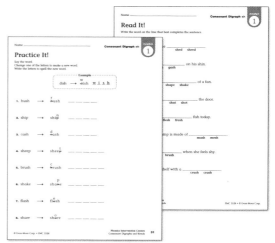

Practice and Assessment Activities

EMC 3526 • © Evan-Moor Corp.

Consonant Digraph sh

Objectives: Students will learn that *s* and *h* together stand for one sound: /sh/.
Students will distinguish the *sh* digraph as an initial or final sound.
Students will blend sounds to read and understand words with the *sh* digraph.

Students' Prior Knowledge: Students can distinguish initial and final sounds.

Introducing the Digraph *sh*

1. Building Phonemic Awareness

Show the front of each sound card for the digraph *sh* as you talk about it. Say:

*The letters **s** and **h** together in a word stand for one sound. The sound is /sh/. Repeat the sound after me: /sh/. (/sh/) You hear /sh/ at the beginning of the word **shin**. You hear /sh/ at the end of the word **wish**.*

Have students listen for the /sh/ sound in the words below. Say:

*Listen carefully to the words I'm going to say. Each word has the /sh/ sound. Say **beginning** or **end** to tell where you hear /sh/ in the word.*

Sound Cards (front)

ship (beg.)	**shoe** (beg.)	**dish** (end)	**shade** (beg.)	**push** (end)
mash (end)	**shred** (beg.)	**cash** (end)	**fresh** (end)	**shampoo** (beg.)

Read each word again and have students repeat it. If needed, stretch the /sh/ sound slightly to help students hear it.

2. Oral Blending

Model oral blending to help students hear the distinct sounds in a word. Say:

*I am going to say a word, sound by sound. Listen: /sh/ /ē/ /p/. The word is **sheep**. Now I am going to say some other words, sound by sound. You blend the sounds for each word and tell me what the word is. Listen:*

/sh/ /ĕ/ /d/ (shed)	/sh/ /ā/ /k/ (shake)	/sh/ /ī/ /n/ (shine)
/r/ /ŭ/ /sh/ (rush)	/tr/ /ă/ /sh/ (trash)	/f/ /ĭ/ /sh/ (fish)

3. Visual Blending

Model visual blending, using the words listed on the back of each sound card. Begin by pointing to the first word and reading it aloud. Then run your finger under the letters as you blend the sounds to read the word again. Repeat this process for the remaining words. For the words **shake** and **shine**, stop before the final *e* and remind students that the *e* has no sound. Next, have students blend the sounds themselves as you run your finger under each letter.

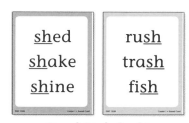

Sound Cards (back)

Consonant Digraph sh *(continued)*

Leading the Center Activities

1. Read, Discriminate, and Identify ....

Give each student Mat A and a set of task cards. Then say:

*We're going to form words that begin or end with the letters **s-h**. Look at the picture in row 1. It shows some cash. Do you hear /sh/ at the beginning of the word **cash** or at the end? (end) Place a card in the box after the letters **c-a**. Now let's blend the sounds and read the word: /k/ /ă/ /sh/ **cash**.*

Repeat this process with the pictures in the remaining rows, or if your students are capable, have them complete the activity with a partner. Give help when needed. Then go over the answers as a group.

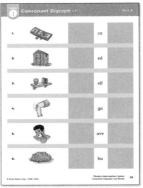

Mat A

2. Read and Understand ....

Have students turn over their mats. Distribute the task cards for Mat B. Then say:

*We're going to form words that name the pictures on this mat. Each word begins or ends with the /sh/ sound. Look at the picture in row 1. It is a ship. Now look at the letters on your cards. Which letters spell the ending of the word **ship**? (i-p) Place the **i-p** card in the box. Now let's blend the sounds and read the word: /sh/ /ĭ/ /p/ **ship**.*

Repeat this process with the pictures in the remaining rows. If your students are capable, have them tell you the names of the pictures rather than you saying them. (brush, shade, shell, dish, trash)

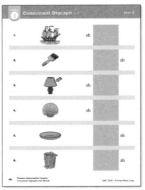

Mat B

3. Practice the Skill ....

Distribute the Practice It! activity (page 31) to students. Read the directions aloud and guide students through the example. Then say:

*Let's blend the sounds to read the first word: /h/ /ŭ/ /sh/ **hush**. Now let's change the letter **h** to an **r** and write the new word: **r-u-s-h**. Now blend the sounds and read the new word: /r/ /ŭ/ /sh/.*

Tell students that as letters change in a word, so do the sounds. Then repeat this process with the remaining words.

Page 31

Apply and Assess

After the lesson, distribute the Read It! activity (page 32) to students and read the directions aloud. Have students complete the activity independently. Then listen to them read the sentences. Use the results as an informal assessment of students' skill mastery.

Page 32

sh

<u>sh</u>in

EMC 3526

sh

wi<u>sh</u>

EMC 3526

Answer Keys

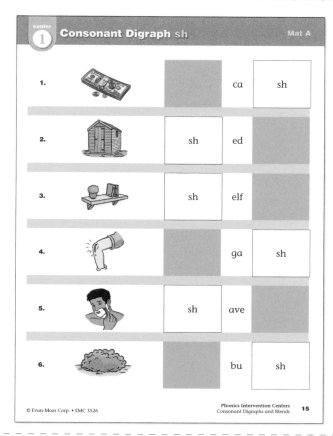

center 1 **Consonant Digraph sh** Mat A

1.			ca	sh
2.		sh	ed	
3.		sh	elf	
4.			ga	sh
5.		sh	ave	
6.			bu	sh

© Evan-Moor Corp. • EMC 3526

Phonics Intervention Centers
Consonant Digraphs and Blends **15**

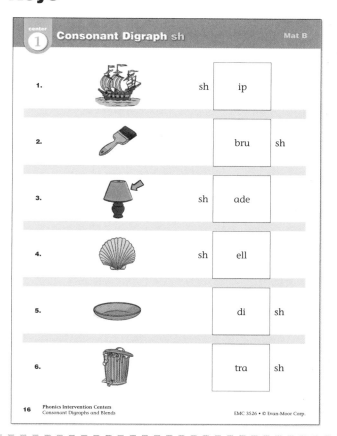

center 1 **Consonant Digraph sh** Mat B

1.		sh	ip
2.		bru	sh
3.		sh	ade
4.		sh	ell
5.		di	sh
6.		tra	sh

16 Phonics Intervention Centers
Consonant Digraphs and Blends

EMC 3526 • © Evan-Moor Corp.

rush
trash
fish

shed
shake
shine

Answer Keys

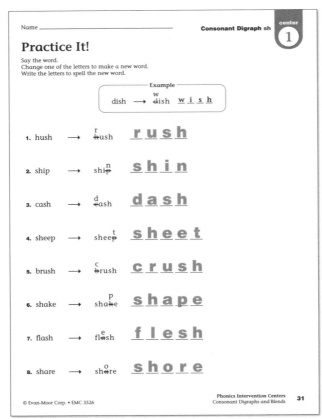

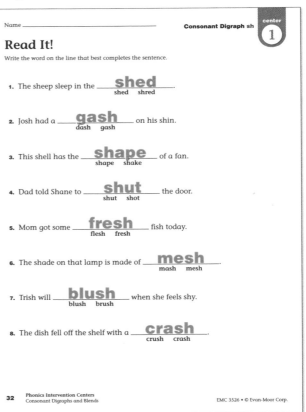

1.

2.

3.

4.

5.

6.

ca

ed

elf

ga

ave

bu

1.  sh

2.  sh

3.  sh

4.  sh

5.  sh

6.  sh

1.

ca

2.

ed

3.

elf

4.

ga

5.

ave

6.

bu

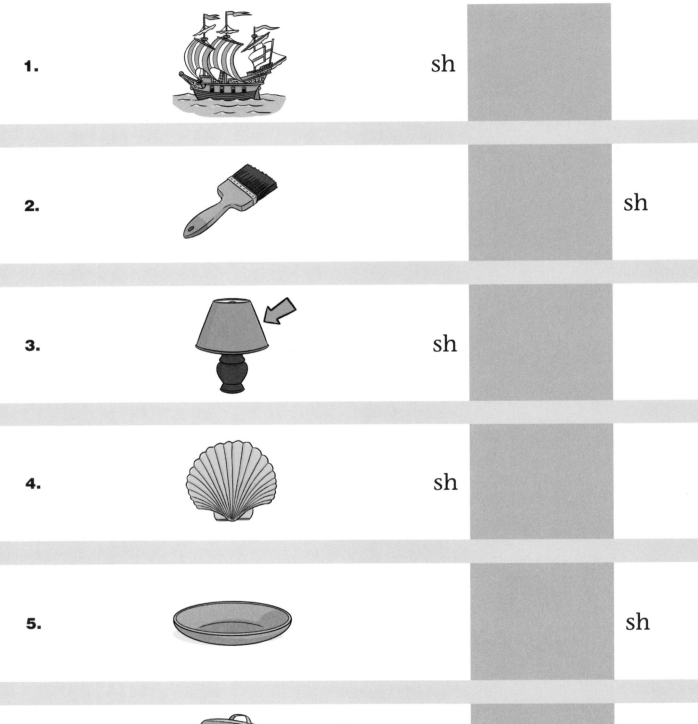

1. sh

2. sh

3. sh

4. sh

5. sh

6. sh

1.

2.

3.

4.

5.

6.

ca

ed

elf

ga

ave

bu

1.  sh

2.  sh

3.  sh

4.  sh

5.  sh

6.  sh

1.

ca

2.

ed

3.

elf

4.

ga

5.

ave

6.

bu

Consonant Digraph sh

1.   sh

2.   sh

3.   sh

4.   sh

5.   sh

6.   sh

EMC 3526 • © Evan-Moor Corp.

1. ca

2. ed

3. elf

4. ga

5. ave

6. bu

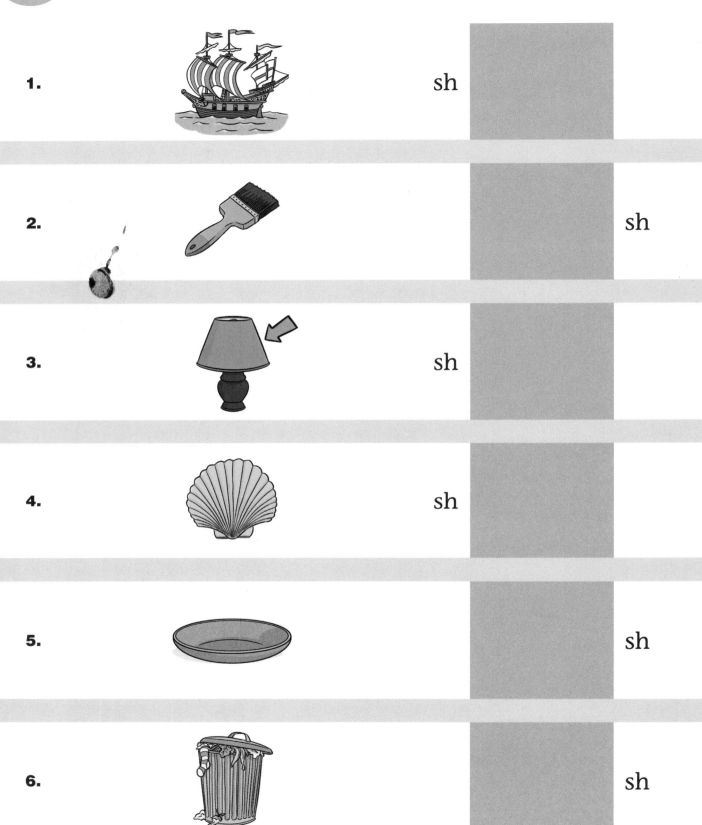

1. sh

2. sh

3. sh

4. sh

5. sh

6. sh

1.

ca

2.

ed

3.

elf

4.

ga

5.

ave

6.

bu

Consonant Digraph sh

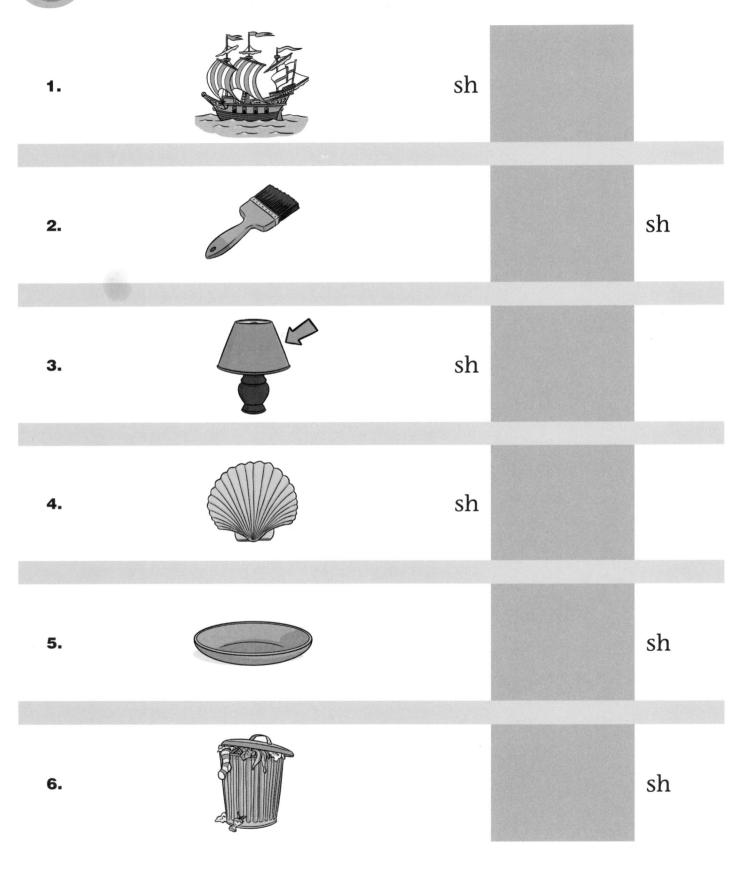

1. sh   sh

2. sh   sh

3. sh   sh

4. sh   sh

5. sh   sh

6. sh   sh

Phonics Intervention Centers
Consonant Digraphs and Blends

EMC 3526 • © Evan-Moor Corp.

Student 6 | sh | sh | sh | sh | sh | sh

Student 5 | sh | sh | sh | sh | sh | sh

Student 4 | sh | sh | sh | sh | sh | sh

Student 3 | sh | sh | sh | sh | sh | sh

Student 2 | sh | sh | sh | sh | sh | sh

Student 1 | sh | sh | sh | sh | sh | sh

Student 6

EMC 3526
Center 1 • Mat A

Student 6

EMC 3526
Center 1 • Mat A

Student 6

EMC 3526
Center 1 • Mat A

Student 6

EMC 3526
Center 1 • Mat A

Student 6

EMC 3526
Center 1 • Mat A

Student 6

EMC 3526
Center 1 • Mat A

Student 5

EMC 3526
Center 1 • Mat A

Student 5

EMC 3526
Center 1 • Mat A

Student 5

EMC 3526
Center 1 • Mat A

Student 5

EMC 3526
Center 1 • Mat A

Student 5

EMC 3526
Center 1 • Mat A

Student 5

EMC 3526
Center 1 • Mat A

Student 4

EMC 3526
Center 1 • Mat A

Student 4

EMC 3526
Center 1 • Mat A

Student 4

EMC 3526
Center 1 • Mat A

Student 4

EMC 3526
Center 1 • Mat A

Student 4

EMC 3526
Center 1 • Mat A

Student 4

EMC 3526
Center 1 • Mat A

Student 3

EMC 3526
Center 1 • Mat A

Student 3

EMC 3526
Center 1 • Mat A

Student 3

EMC 3526
Center 1 • Mat A

Student 3

EMC 3526
Center 1 • Mat A

Student 3

EMC 3526
Center 1 • Mat A

Student 3

EMC 3526
Center 1 • Mat A

Student 2

EMC 3526
Center 1 • Mat A

Student 2

EMC 3526
Center 1 • Mat A

Student 2

EMC 3526
Center 1 • Mat A

Student 2

EMC 3526
Center 1 • Mat A

Student 2

EMC 3526
Center 1 • Mat A

Student 2

EMC 3526
Center 1 • Mat A

Student 1

EMC 3526
Center 1 • Mat A

Student 1

EMC 3526
Center 1 • Mat A

Student 1

EMC 3526
Center 1 • Mat A

Student 1

EMC 3526
Center 1 • Mat A

Student 1

EMC 3526
Center 1 • Mat A

Student 1

EMC 3526
Center 1 • Mat A

Student 6	ade	bru	di	ell	ip	tra
Student 5	ade	bru	di	ell	ip	tra
Student 4	ade	bru	di	ell	ip	tra
Student 3	ade	bru	di	ell	ip	tra
Student 2	ade	bru	di	ell	ip	tra
Student 1	ade	bru	di	ell	ip	tra

Student 6 EMC 3526 Center 1 • Mat B	**Student 5** EMC 3526 Center 1 • Mat B	**Student 4** EMC 3526 Center 1 • Mat B
Student 6 EMC 3526 Center 1 • Mat B	**Student 5** EMC 3526 Center 1 • Mat B	**Student 3** EMC 3526 Center 1 • Mat B
Student 6 EMC 3526 Center 1 • Mat B	**Student 5** EMC 3526 Center 1 • Mat B	**Student 3** EMC 3526 Center 1 • Mat B
Student 6 EMC 3526 Center 1 • Mat B	**Student 5** EMC 3526 Center 1 • Mat B	**Student 3** EMC 3526 Center 1 • Mat B
Student 6 EMC 3526 Center 1 • Mat B	**Student 5** EMC 3526 Center 1 • Mat B	**Student 3** EMC 3526 Center 1 • Mat B
Student 6 EMC 3526 Center 1 • Mat B	**Student 5** EMC 3526 Center 1 • Mat B	**Student 3** EMC 3526 Center 1 • Mat B
Student 6 EMC 3526 Center 1 • Mat B	**Student 5** EMC 3526 Center 1 • Mat B	**Student 3** EMC 3526 Center 1 • Mat B

Student 4 EMC 3526 Center 1 • Mat B	**Student 2** EMC 3526 Center 1 • Mat B	
Student 4 EMC 3526 Center 1 • Mat B	**Student 2** EMC 3526 Center 1 • Mat B	
Student 4 EMC 3526 Center 1 • Mat B	**Student 2** EMC 3526 Center 1 • Mat B	
Student 4 EMC 3526 Center 1 • Mat B	**Student 2** EMC 3526 Center 1 • Mat B	
Student 4 EMC 3526 Center 1 • Mat B	**Student 2** EMC 3526 Center 1 • Mat B	
Student 3 EMC 3526 Center 1 • Mat B	**Student 1** EMC 3526 Center 1 • Mat B	
Student 2 EMC 3526 Center 1 • Mat B	**Student 1** EMC 3526 Center 1 • Mat B	
Student 2 EMC 3526 Center 1 • Mat B	**Student 1** EMC 3526 Center 1 • Mat B	
Student 2 EMC 3526 Center 1 • Mat B	**Student 1** EMC 3526 Center 1 • Mat B	
Student 1 EMC 3526 Center 1 • Mat B		

Practice It!

Say the word.
Change one of the letters to make a new word.
Write the letters to spell the new word.

> **Example**
>
> dish ⟶ w̶dish __w__ __i__ __s__ __h__

1. hush ⟶ r̶hush   r u s h

2. ship ⟶ ship n̶   s h i n

3. cash ⟶ d̶eash   d a s h

4. sheep ⟶ sheep t̶   s h e e t

5. brush ⟶ c̶brush   c r u s h

6. shake ⟶ sha p̶ke   s h a p e

7. flash ⟶ fl e̶ash   f l e s h

8. share ⟶ sh o̶are   s h o r e

Read It!

Write the word on the line that best completes the sentence.

1. The sheep sleep in the ___*shed*___.
   (shed)   shred

2. Josh had a ___*gash*___ on his shin.
   dash   (gash)

3. This shell has the ___*shape*___ of a fan.
   (shape)   shake

4. Dad told Shane to ___*shut*___ the door.
   (shut)   shot

5. Mom got some ___*fresh*___ fish today.
   flesh   (fresh)

6. The shade on that lamp is made of ___*mesh*___.
   mash   (mesh)

7. Trish will ___*blush*___ when she feels shy.
   (blush)   brush

8. The dish fell off the shelf with a ___*crash*___.
   crush   (crash)

center 2

Consonant Digraph ch

For the Teacher

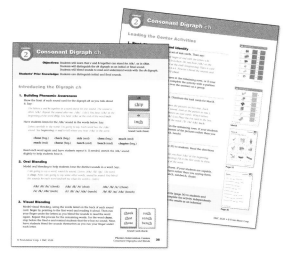

Lesson Plan

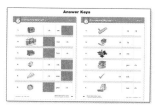

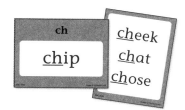

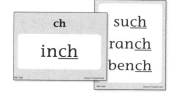

Sound Cards

Answer Keys

For the Student

front (Mat A)

back (Mat B)

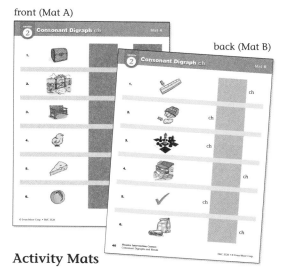

Activity Mats

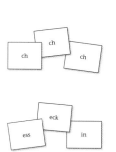

Task Cards

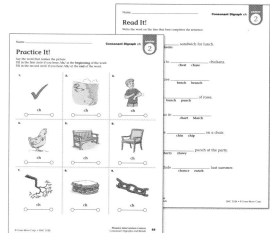

Practice and Assessment Activities

Consonant Digraph ch

Objectives: Students will learn that *c* and *h* together can stand for /ch/, as in **chin**.
Students will distinguish the *ch* digraph as an initial or final sound.
Students will blend sounds to read and understand words with the *ch* digraph.

Students' Prior Knowledge: Students can distinguish initial and final sounds.

Introducing the Digraph *ch*

1. Building Phonemic Awareness

Show the front of each sound card for the digraph *ch* as you talk about it. Say:

The letters c and h together in a word stand for one sound. The sound is often /ch/. Repeat the sound after me: /ch/. (/ch/) You hear /ch/ at the beginning of the word **chip.** *You hear /ch/ at the end of the word* **inch.**

Have students listen for the /ch/ sound in the words below. Say:

Listen carefully to the words I'm going to say. Each word has the /ch/ sound. Say **beginning** *or* **end** *to tell where you hear /ch/ in the word.*

Sound Cards (front)

chase (beg.)	**check** (beg.)	**rich** (end)	**chess** (beg.)	**much** (end)
reach (end)	**cheese** (beg.)	**lunch** (end)	**beach** (end)	**chapter** (beg.)

Read each word again and have students repeat it. If needed, stretch the /ch/ sound slightly to help students hear it.

2. Oral Blending

Model oral blending to help students hear the distinct sounds in a word. Say:

I am going to say a word, sound by sound. Listen: /ch/ /ŏ/ /p/. The word is **chop.** *Now I am going to say some other words, sound by sound. You blend the sounds for each word and tell me what the word is. Listen:*

/ch/ /ē/ /k/ (cheek)	/ch/ /ă/ /t/ (chat)	/ch/ /ō/ /z/ (chose)
/s/ /ŭ/ /ch/ (such)	/r/ /ă/ /n/ /ch/ (ranch)	/b/ /ĕ/ /n/ /ch/ (bench)

3. Visual Blending

Model visual blending, using the words listed on the back of each sound card. Begin by pointing to the first word and reading it aloud. Then run your finger under the letters as you blend the sounds to read the word again. Repeat this process for the remaining words. For the word **chose,** stop before the final *e* and remind students that the *e* has no sound. Next, have students blend the sounds themselves as you run your finger under each letter.

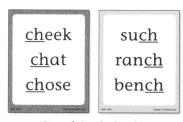

Sound Cards (back)

Leading the Center Activities

1. Read, Discriminate, and Identify ....

Give each student Mat A and a set of task cards. Then say:

*We're going to form words that begin or end with the letters c-h. Look at the picture in row 1. It is a chest. Do you hear /ch/ at the beginning of the word **chest** or at the end? (beginning) Place a card in the box in front of the letters e-s-t. Now let's blend the sounds and read the word: /ch/ /ĕ/ /s/ /t/ chest.*

Repeat this process with the pictures in the remaining rows, or if your students are capable, have them complete the activity with a partner. Give help when needed. Then go over the answers as a group.

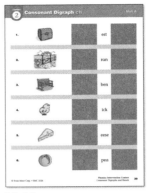

Mat A

2. Read and Understand ....

Have students turn over their mats. Distribute the task cards for Mat B. Then say:

*We're going to form words that name the pictures on this mat. Each word begins or ends with the /ch/ sound. Look at the picture in row 1. It shows an inch. Now look at the letters on your cards. Which letters spell the beginning of the word **inch**? (i-n) Place the i-n card in the box. Now let's blend the sounds and read the word: /ĭ/ /n/ /ch/ inch.*

Repeat this process with the pictures in the remaining rows. If your students are capable, have them tell you the names of the pictures rather than you saying them. (chip, chess, porch, check, lunch)

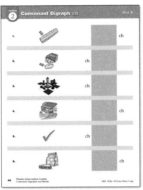

Mat B

3. Practice the Skill ....

Distribute the Practice It! activity (page 55) to students. Read the directions aloud. Then say:

*Look at the first picture. It is a check. Do you hear /ch/ at the beginning of the word **check** or at the end? (beginning) Fill in the first circle to show that the letters c-h are at the beginning of the word.*

Repeat this process for the remaining pictures. If your students are capable, have them tell you the names of the pictures rather than you saying them. (beach, pinch, chicken, bench, chair, branch, sandwich, chain)

Page 55

Apply and Assess

After the lesson, distribute the Read It! activity (page 56) to students and read the directions aloud. Have students complete the activity independently. Then listen to them read the sentences. Use the results as an informal assessment of students' skill mastery.

Page 56

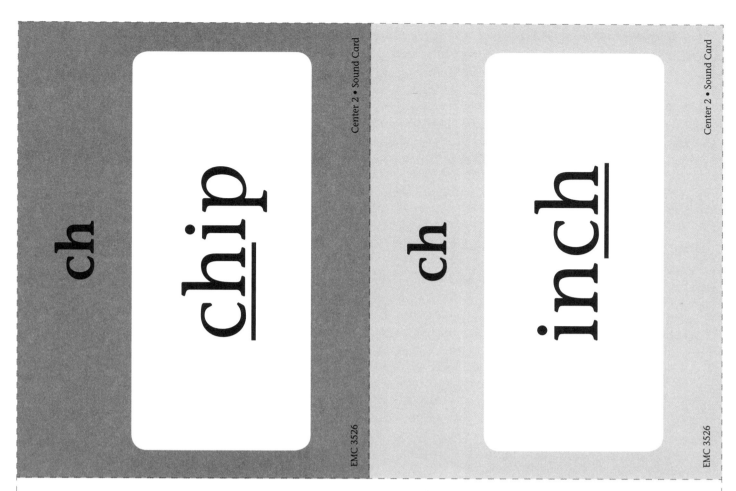

ch

ch<u>ip</u>

ch

in<u>ch</u>

EMC 3526

EMC 3526

Answer Keys

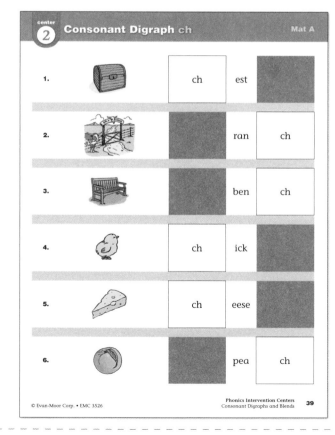

1. | ch | est |
2. | ran | ch |
3. | ben | ch |
4. | ch | ick |
5. | ch | eese |
6. | pea | ch |

Phonics Intervention Centers
Consonant Digraphs and Blends **39**

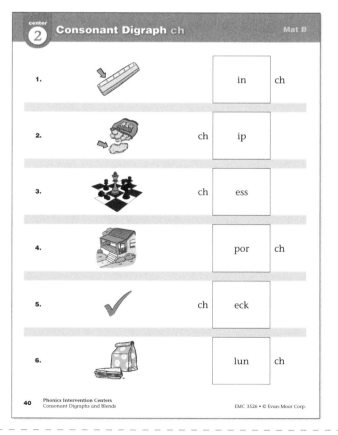

1. | in | ch |
2. | ch | ip |
3. | ch | ess |
4. | por | ch |
5. | ch | eck |
6. | lun | ch |

such
ranch
bench

Center 2 • Sound Card

cheek
chat
chose

Center 2 • Sound Card

Answer Keys

1. 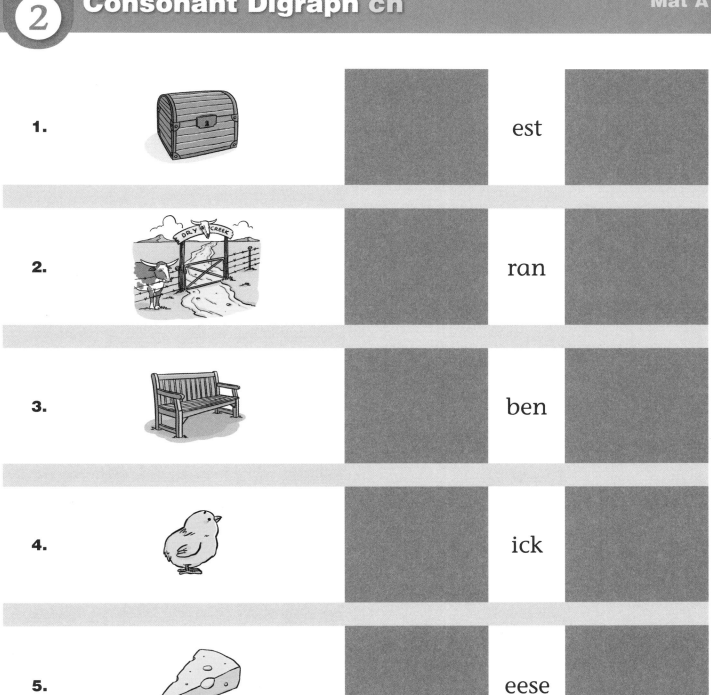 est

2. ran

3. ben

4. ick

5. eese

6. pea

1.  ch

2.  ch

3.  ch

4.  ch

5. ch

6.  ch

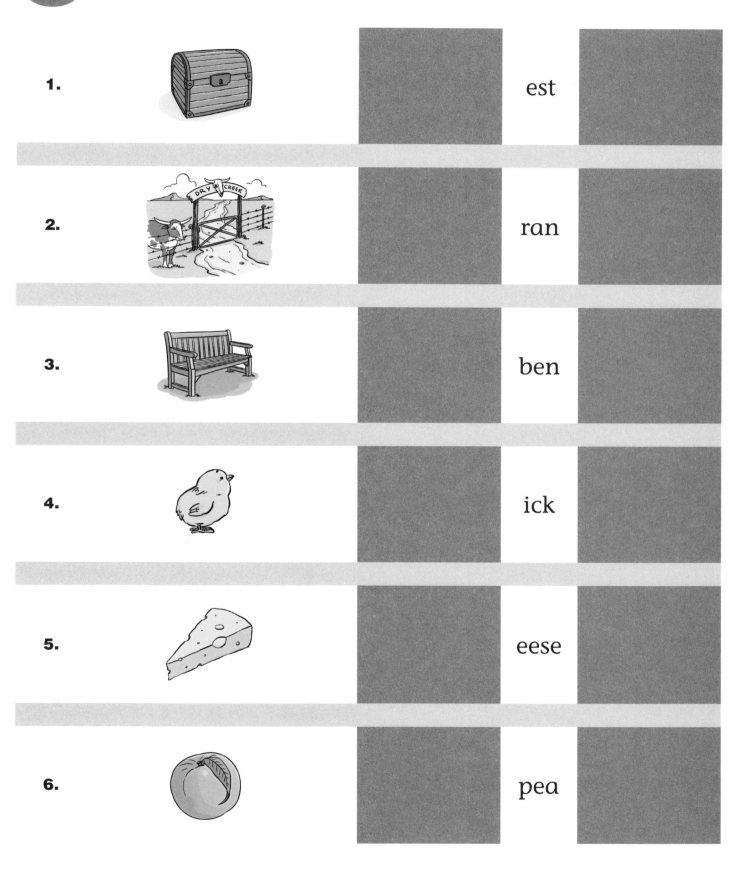

1.

2.

3.

est

ran

ben

ick

eese

pea

4.

5.

6.

1.  ch

2.  ch

3.  ch

4.  ch

5. ch

6.  ch

Phonics Intervention Centers
Consonant Digraphs and Blends

EMC 3526 • © Evan-Moor Corp.

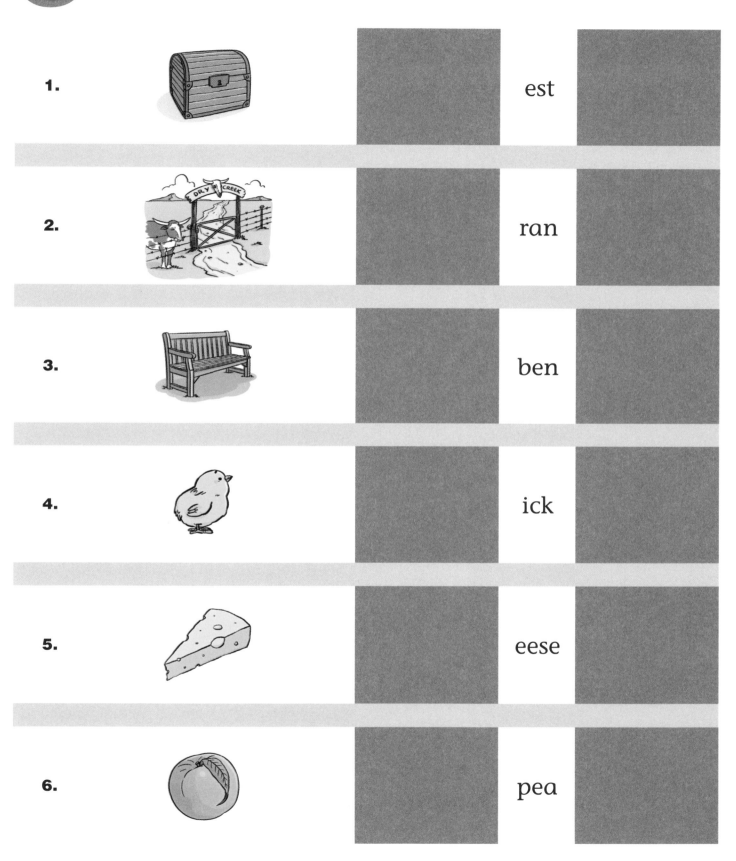

1. est

2. ran

3. ben

4. ick

5. eese

6. pea

1.  ch

2.  ch

3.  ch

4.  ch

5. ch

6.  ch

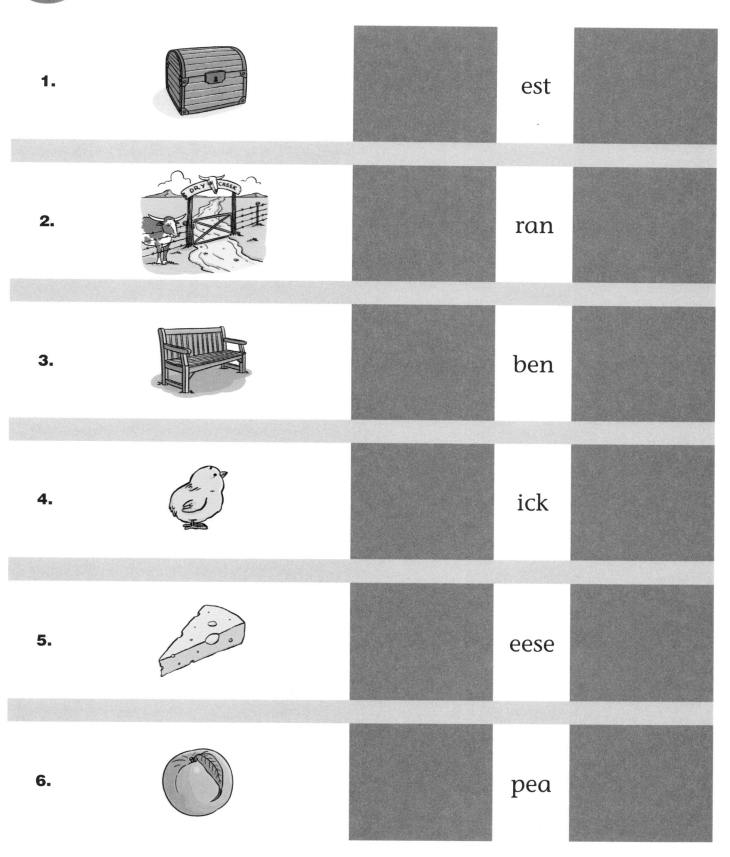

1. est

2. ran

3. ben

4. ick

5. eese

6. pea

1.  ch

2. ch

3.  ch

4.  ch

5.  ch

6.  ch

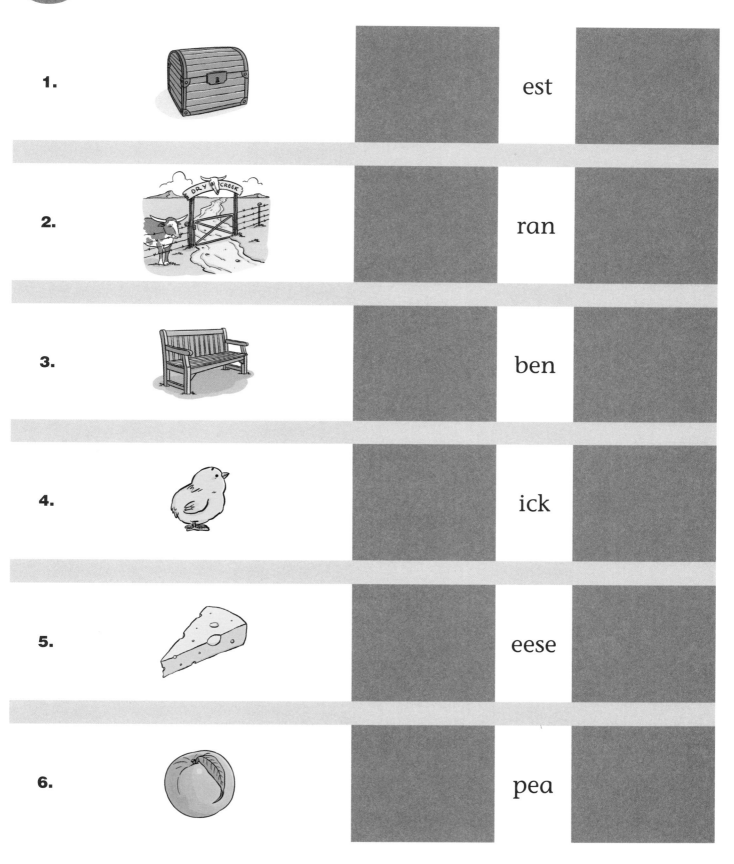

1. est

2. ran

3. ben

4. ick

5. eese

6. pea

1.  ch

2.  ch

3.  ch

4.  ch

5. ch

6.  ch

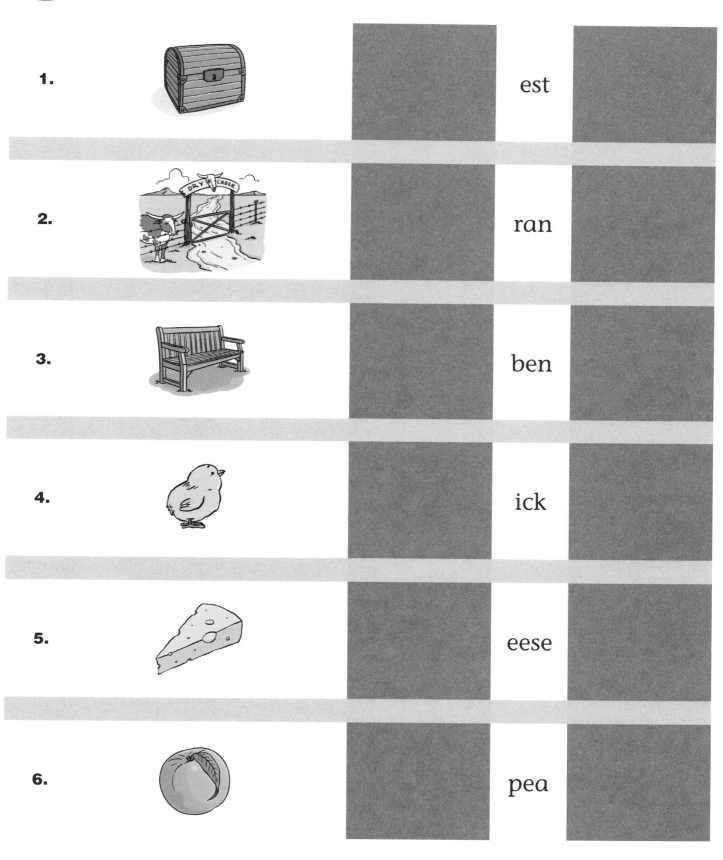

1. est

2. ran

3. ben

4. ick

5. eese

6. pea

1.  ch

2.  ch

3.  ch

4.  ch

5. ch

6.  ch

Student 6	ch	ch	ch	ch	ch	ch
Student 5	ch	ch	ch	ch	ch	ch
Student 4	ch	ch	ch	ch	ch	ch
Student 3	ch	ch	ch	ch	ch	ch
Student 2	ch	ch	ch	ch	ch	ch
Student 1	ch	ch	ch	ch	ch	ch

Student 6

EMC 3526
Center 2 • Mat A

Student 6

EMC 3526
Center 2 • Mat A

Student 6

EMC 3526
Center 2 • Mat A

Student 6

EMC 3526
Center 2 • Mat A

Student 6

EMC 3526
Center 2 • Mat A

Student 6

EMC 3526
Center 2 • Mat A

Student 5

EMC 3526
Center 2 • Mat A

Student 5

EMC 3526
Center 2 • Mat A

Student 5

EMC 3526
Center 2 • Mat A

Student 5

EMC 3526
Center 2 • Mat A

Student 5

EMC 3526
Center 2 • Mat A

Student 5

EMC 3526
Center 2 • Mat A

Student 4

EMC 3526
Center 2 • Mat A

Student 4

EMC 3526
Center 2 • Mat A

Student 4

EMC 3526
Center 2 • Mat A

Student 4

EMC 3526
Center 2 • Mat A

Student 4

EMC 3526
Center 2 • Mat A

Student 4

EMC 3526
Center 2 • Mat A

Student 3

EMC 3526
Center 2 • Mat A

Student 3

EMC 3526
Center 2 • Mat A

Student 3

EMC 3526
Center 2 • Mat A

Student 3

EMC 3526
Center 2 • Mat A

Student 3

EMC 3526
Center 2 • Mat A

Student 3

EMC 3526
Center 2 • Mat A

Student 2

EMC 3526
Center 2 • Mat A

Student 2

EMC 3526
Center 2 • Mat A

Student 2

EMC 3526
Center 2 • Mat A

Student 2

EMC 3526
Center 2 • Mat A

Student 2

EMC 3526
Center 2 • Mat A

Student 2

EMC 3526
Center 2 • Mat A

Student 1

EMC 3526
Center 2 • Mat A

Student 1

EMC 3526
Center 2 • Mat A

Student 1

EMC 3526
Center 2 • Mat A

Student 1

EMC 3526
Center 2 • Mat A

Student 1

EMC 3526
Center 2 • Mat A

Student 1

EMC 3526
Center 2 • Mat A

Student 6	Student 5	Student 4	Student 3	Student 2	Student 1
eck	eck	eck	eck	eck	eck
ess	ess	ess	ess	ess	ess
in	in	in	in	in	in
ip	ip	ip	ip	ip	ip
lun	lun	lun	lun	lun	lun
por	por	por	por	por	por

Student 6

EMC 3526
Center 2 • Mat B

Student 6

EMC 3526
Center 2 • Mat B

Student 6

EMC 3526
Center 2 • Mat B

Student 6

EMC 3526
Center 2 • Mat B

Student 6

EMC 3526
Center 2 • Mat B

Student 6

EMC 3526
Center 2 • Mat B

Student 5

EMC 3526
Center 2 • Mat B

Student 5

EMC 3526
Center 2 • Mat B

Student 5

EMC 3526
Center 2 • Mat B

Student 5

EMC 3526
Center 2 • Mat B

Student 5

EMC 3526
Center 2 • Mat B

Student 5

EMC 3526
Center 2 • Mat B

Student 4

EMC 3526
Center 2 • Mat B

Student 4

EMC 3526
Center 2 • Mat B

Student 4

EMC 3526
Center 2 • Mat B

Student 4

EMC 3526
Center 2 • Mat B

Student 4

EMC 3526
Center 2 • Mat B

Student 4

EMC 3526
Center 2 • Mat B

Student 3

EMC 3526
Center 2 • Mat B

Student 3

EMC 3526
Center 2 • Mat B

Student 3

EMC 3526
Center 2 • Mat B

Student 3

EMC 3526
Center 2 • Mat B

Student 3

EMC 3526
Center 2 • Mat B

Student 3

EMC 3526
Center 2 • Mat B

Student 2

EMC 3526
Center 2 • Mat B

Student 2

EMC 3526
Center 2 • Mat B

Student 2

EMC 3526
Center 2 • Mat B

Student 2

EMC 3526
Center 2 • Mat B

Student 2

EMC 3526
Center 2 • Mat B

Student 2

EMC 3526
Center 2 • Mat B

Student 1

EMC 3526
Center 2 • Mat B

Student 1

EMC 3526
Center 2 • Mat B

Student 1

EMC 3526
Center 2 • Mat B

Student 1

EMC 3526
Center 2 • Mat B

Student 1

EMC 3526
Center 2 • Mat B

Student 1

EMC 3526
Center 2 • Mat B

Practice It!

Say the word that names the picture.
Fill in the first circle if you hear **/ch/** at the **beginning** of the word.
Fill in the second circle if you hear **/ch/** at the **end** of the word.

1.

ch

○——○

2.

ch

○——○

3.

ch

○——○

4.

ch

○——○

5.

ch

○——○

6.

ch

○——○

7.

ch

○——○

8.

ch

○——○

9.

ch

○——○

Read It!

Write the word on the line that best completes the sentence.

1. I ate a ____Cheese____ sandwich for lunch.
   cheese   cheeks

2. My cat Cheetah likes to _____ chickens.
   chest   chase

3. The chimp sat on a tree _____.
   bench   branch

4. Dad gave Mom a _____ of roses.
   bunch   punch

5. Chan will go to China in _____.
   chart   March

6. Chuck fell and hit his _____ on a chair.
   chin   chip

7. I had a glass of _____ punch at the party.
   cherry   chewy

8. We chose to go to a dude _____ last summer.
   chance   ranch

center 3

Consonant Digraph th

For the Teacher

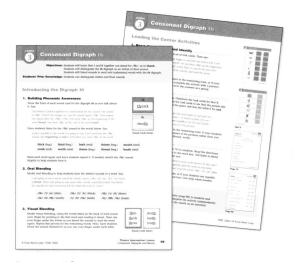

Lesson Plan

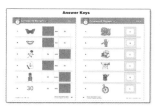

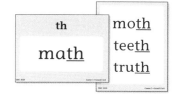

Sound Cards

Answer Keys

For the Student

front (Mat A)

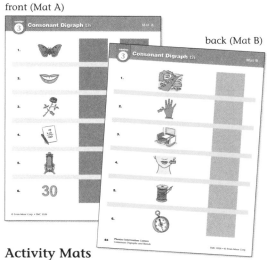

back (Mat B)

Activity Mats

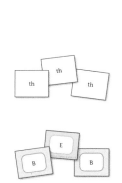

Task Cards

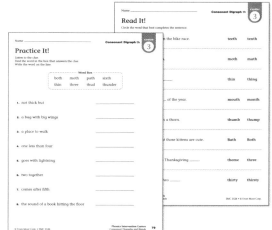

Practice and Assessment Activities

Phonics Intervention Centers
Consonant Digraphs and Blends

EMC 3526 • © Evan-Moor Corp.

Consonant Digraph th

Objectives: Students will learn that *t* and *h* together can stand for /th/, as in **thank**.

Students will distinguish the *th* digraph as an initial or final sound.

Students will blend sounds to read and understand words with the *th* digraph.

Students' Prior Knowledge: Students can distinguish initial and final sounds.

Introducing the Digraph *th*

1. Building Phonemic Awareness

Show the front of each sound card for the digraph **th** as you talk about it. Say:

*The letters **t** and **h** together in a word stand for one sound. The sound is /th/. Watch my tongue as I say the sound again: /th/. Now repeat the sound after me: /th/. (/th/) You hear /th/ at the beginning of the word **thank**. You hear /th/ at the end of the word **math**.*

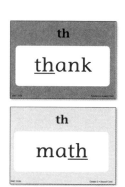

Sound Cards (front)

Have students listen for the /th/ sound in the words below. Say:

*Listen carefully to the words I'm going to say. Each word has the /th/ sound. Say **beginning** or **end** to tell where you hear /th/ in the word.*

thick (beg.)	**third** (beg.)	**bath** (end)	**thirsty** (beg.)	**mouth** (end)
south (end)	**worth** (end)	**theme** (beg.)	**thread** (beg.)	**booth** (end)

Read each word again and have students repeat it. If needed, stretch the /th/ sound slightly to help students hear it.

2. Oral Blending

Model oral blending to help students hear the distinct sounds in a word. Say:

*I am going to say a word, sound by sound. Listen: /th/ /ĭ/ /n/ /k/. The word is **think**. Now I am going to say some other words, sound by sound. You blend the sounds for each word and tell me what the word is. Listen:*

/th/ /ĭ/ /n/ (thin)	/th/ /ĭ/ /k/ (thick)	/th/ /r/ /ē/ (three)
/m/ /ŏ/ /th/ (moth)	/t/ /ē/ /th/ (teeth)	/tr/ /o͞o/ /th/ (truth)

3. Visual Blending

Model visual blending, using the words listed on the back of each sound card. Begin by pointing to the first word and reading it aloud. Then run your finger under the letters as you blend the sounds to read the word again. Repeat this process for the remaining words. Next, have students blend the sounds themselves as you run your finger under each letter.

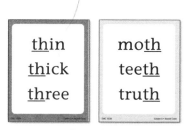

thin	moth
thick	teeth
three	truth

Sound Cards (back)

Leading the Center Activities

1. Read, Discriminate, and Identify ....

Give each student Mat A and a set of task cards. Then say:

*We're going to form words that begin or end with the letters **t-h**. Look at the picture in row 1. It is a moth. Do you hear /**th**/ at the beginning of the word **moth** or at the end? (end) Place a card in the box after the letters **m-o**. Now let's blend the sounds and read the word: /m/ /ŏ/ /**th**/ **moth**.*

Repeat this process with the pictures in the remaining rows, or if your students are capable, have them complete the activity with a partner. Give help when needed. Then go over the answers as a group.

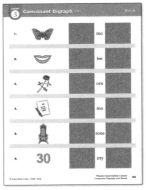

Mat A

2. Read and Understand ....

Have students turn over their mats. Distribute the task cards for Mat B. Tell students to look at both sides of the task cards to see that the purple side has the letter **B** for **beginning**, and the green side has the letter **E** for **end**. Then say:

*The words that name the pictures on this mat begin or end with the /**th**/ sound. Look at the picture in row 1. It shows a path. Do you hear /**th**/ at the beginning of the word **path** or at the end? (end) Place the letter **E** for **end** in the box next to the picture.*

Repeat this process with the pictures in the remaining rows. If your students are capable, have them tell you the names of the pictures rather than you saying them. (thumb, booth, mouth, thread, north)

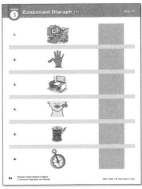

Mat B

3. Practice the Skill ....

Distribute the Practice It! activity (page 79) to students. Read the directions aloud and have students say the words in the word box. Tell them to blend the sounds as they read each word. Then say:

*Listen to the first clue: **not thick but**. Which word is the answer to this clue? (thin) Write **thin** on the line. You may quietly spell the word as you write the letters. Now let's blend the sounds and read the word: /**th**/ /ĭ/ /n/ **thin**.*

Repeat this process for the remaining clues, or if your students are capable, have them complete the activity with a partner. Give help when needed. Then go over the answers as a group.

Page 79

Apply and Assess

After the lesson, distribute the Read It! activity (page 80) to students and read the directions aloud. Have students complete the activity independently. Then listen to them read the sentences. Use the results as an informal assessment of students' skill mastery.

Page 80

th

th**ank**

ma**th**

EMC 3526

Answer Keys

center 3 — **Consonant Digraph th** — Mat A

1. mo | th
2. tee | th
3. th | orn
4. ma | th
5. th | rone
6. 30 — th | irty

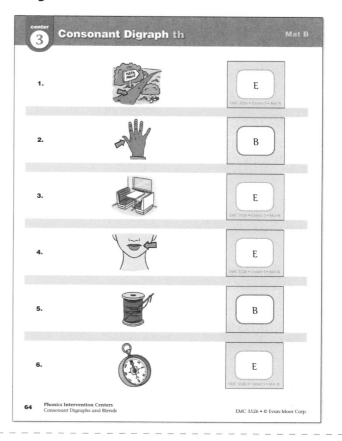

center 3 — **Consonant Digraph th** — Mat B

1. E
2. B
3. E
4. E
5. B
6. E

moth

teeth

truth

Center 3 • Sound Card

thin

thick

three

Center 3 • Sound Card

Answer Keys

Name _____

Consonant Digraph th

center **3**

Practice It!

Listen to the clue.
Find the word in the box that answers the clue.
Write the word on the line.

┌─── Word Box ───┐
both   moth   path   sixth
thin   three   thud   thunder

1. not thick but **thin**

2. a bug with big wings **moth**

3. a place to walk **path**

4. one less than four **three**

5. goes with lightning **thunder**

6. two together **both**

7. comes after fifth **sixth**

8. the sound of a book hitting the floor **thud**

© Evan-Moor Corp. • EMC 3526

Phonics Intervention Centers
Consonant Digraphs and Blends   **79**

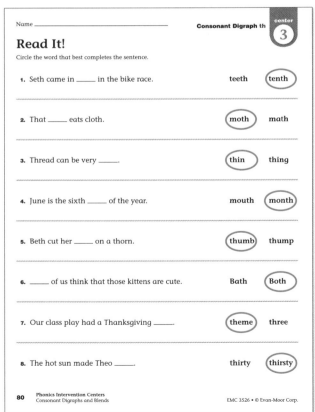

Name _____

Consonant Digraph th

center **3**

Read It!

Circle the word that best completes the sentence.

1. Seth came in _____ in the bike race.   teeth   (tenth)

2. That _____ eats cloth.   (moth)   math

3. Thread can be very _____.   (thin)   thing

4. June is the sixth _____ of the year.   mouth   (month)

5. Beth cut her _____ on a thorn.   (thumb)   thump

6. _____ of us think that those kittens are cute.   Bath   (Both)

7. Our class play had a Thanksgiving _____.   (theme)   three

8. The hot sun made Theo _____.   thirty   (thirsty)

80   Phonics Intervention Centers
Consonant Digraphs and Blends   EMC 3526 • © Evan-Moor Corp.

1. | mo

2. | tee

3. | orn

4. | ma

5. | rone

6. | irty

1.

2.

3.

4.

5.

6.

1. mo

2. tee

3. orn

4. ma

5. rone

6. irty

1.

2.

3.

4.

5.

6.

1.

mo

2.

tee

3.

orn

4.

ma

5.

rone

6. 30

irty

1.

2.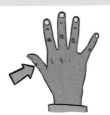

3.

4.

5.

6.

1. mo

2. tee

3. orn

4. ma

5. rone

6. irty

1.

2.

3.

4.

5.

6.

Phonics Intervention Centers
Consonant Digraphs and Blends

EMC 3526 • © Evan-Moor Corp.

1. mo

2. tee

3. orn

4. ma

5. rone

6. irty

1.

2.

3.

4.

5.

6.

Phonics Intervention Centers
Consonant Digraphs and Blends

EMC 3526 • © Evan-Moor Corp.

1.   mo

2.   tee

3.   orn

4.   ma

5.   rone

6. **30**   irty

1.

2.

3.

4.

5.

6.

Phonics Intervention Centers
Consonant Digraphs and Blends

Student 6	th	th	th	th	th	th
Student 5	th	th	th	th	th	th
Student 4	th	th	th	th	th	th
Student 3	th	th	th	th	th	th
Student 2	th	th	th	th	th	th
Student 1	th	th	th	th	th	th

Student 6

EMC 3526
Center 3 • Mat A

Student 6

EMC 3526
Center 3 • Mat A

Student 6

EMC 3526
Center 3 • Mat A

Student 6

EMC 3526
Center 3 • Mat A

Student 6

EMC 3526
Center 3 • Mat A

Student 6

EMC 3526
Center 3 • Mat A

Student 5

EMC 3526
Center 3 • Mat A

Student 5

EMC 3526
Center 3 • Mat A

Student 5

EMC 3526
Center 3 • Mat A

Student 5

EMC 3526
Center 3 • Mat A

Student 5

EMC 3526
Center 3 • Mat A

Student 5

EMC 3526
Center 3 • Mat A

Student 4

EMC 3526
Center 3 • Mat A

Student 4

EMC 3526
Center 3 • Mat A

Student 4

EMC 3526
Center 3 • Mat A

Student 4

EMC 3526
Center 3 • Mat A

Student 4

EMC 3526
Center 3 • Mat A

Student 4

EMC 3526
Center 3 • Mat A

Student 3

EMC 3526
Center 3 • Mat A

Student 3

EMC 3526
Center 3 • Mat A

Student 3

EMC 3526
Center 3 • Mat A

Student 3

EMC 3526
Center 3 • Mat A

Student 3

EMC 3526
Center 3 • Mat A

Student 3

EMC 3526
Center 3 • Mat A

Student 2

EMC 3526
Center 3 • Mat A

Student 2

EMC 3526
Center 3 • Mat A

Student 2

EMC 3526
Center 3 • Mat A

Student 2

EMC 3526
Center 3 • Mat A

Student 2

EMC 3526
Center 3 • Mat A

Student 2

EMC 3526
Center 3 • Mat A

Student 1

EMC 3526
Center 3 • Mat A

Student 1

EMC 3526
Center 3 • Mat A

Student 1

EMC 3526
Center 3 • Mat A

Student 1

EMC 3526
Center 3 • Mat A

Student 1

EMC 3526
Center 3 • Mat A

Student 1

EMC 3526
Center 3 • Mat A

Student 6	Student 5	Student 4	Student 3	Student 2	Student 1
B	B	B	B	B	B
B	B	B	B	B	B
B	B	B	B	B	B
B	B	B	B	B	B
B	B	B	B	B	B
B	B	B	B	B	B

Phonics Intervention Centers
Consonant Digraphs and Blends

EMC 3526 • © Evan-Moor Corp.

Practice It!

Listen to the clue.
Find the word in the box that answers the clue.
Write the word on the line.

─── **Word Box** ───

| both | moth | path | sixth |
| thin | three | thud | thunder |

1. not thick but _____

2. a bug with big wings _____

3. a place to walk _____

4. one less than four _____

5. goes with lightning _____

6. two together _____

7. comes after fifth _____

8. the sound of a book hitting the floor _____

Read It!

Circle the word that best completes the sentence.

1. Seth came in _____ in the bike race.   teeth   tenth

2. That _____ eats cloth.   moth   math

3. Thread can be very _____.   thin   thing

4. June is the sixth _____ of the year.   mouth   month

5. Beth cut her _____ on a thorn.   thumb   thump

6. _____ of us think that those kittens are cute.   Bath   Both

7. Our class play had a Thanksgiving _____.   theme   three

8. The hot sun made Theo _____.   thirty   thirsty

INTERMEDIATE

Consonant Digraphs Review

For the Teacher

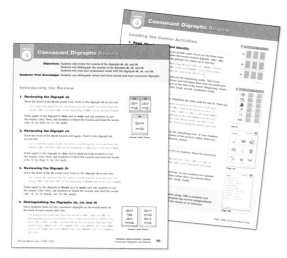

Lesson Plan

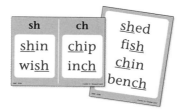

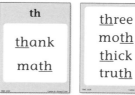

Sound Cards

Answer Keys

For the Student

front (Mat A)

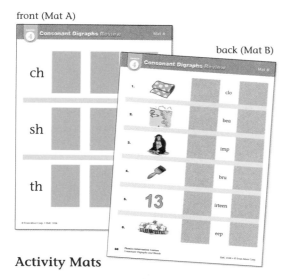

back (Mat B)

Activity Mats

Task Cards

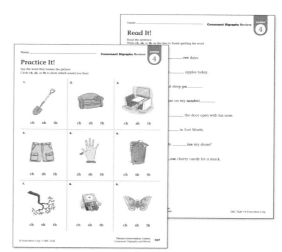

Practice and Assessment Activities

Consonant Digraphs Review

Objectives: Students will review the sounds of the digraphs *sh*, *ch*, and *th*.
Students will distinguish the sounds of the digraphs *sh*, *ch*, and *th*.
Students will read and understand words with the digraphs *sh*, *ch*, and *th*.

Students' Prior Knowledge: Students can distinguish initial and final sounds and read consonant digraphs.

Introducing the Review

1. Reviewing the Digraph *sh*

Show the front of the **sh/ch** sound card. Point to the digraph **sh** as you say:

Let's review the sound of s-h. The letters s and h together in a word have this sound: /sh/. You hear /sh/ at the beginning of shin and at the end of wish.

Point again to the digraph in **shin** and in **wish** and ask students to say the sound. (/sh/) Next, ask students to blend the sounds and read the words. (/sh/ /ĭ/ /n/ shin; /w/ /ĭ/ /sh/ wish)

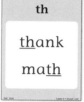

Sound Cards (front)

2. Reviewing the Digraph *ch*

Show the front of the **sh/ch** sound card again. Point to the digraph **ch** as you say:

Let's review the sound of c-h. The letters c and h together in a word have this sound: /ch/. You hear /ch/ at the beginning of chip and at the end of inch.

Point again to the digraph in **chip** and in **inch** and ask students to say the sound. (/ch/) Next, ask students to blend the sounds and read the words. (/ch/ /ĭ/ /p/ chip; /ĭ/ /n/ /ch/ inch)

3. Reviewing the Digraph *th*

Show the front of the **th** sound card. Point to the digraph **th** as you say:

Let's review the sound of t-h. The letters t and h together in a word have this sound: /th/. You hear /th/ at the beginning of thank and at the end of math.

Point again to the digraph in **thank** and in **math** and ask students to say the sound. (/th/) Next, ask students to blend the sounds and read the words. (/th/ /ă/ /n/ /k/ thank; /m/ /ă/ /th/ math)

4. Distinguishing the Digraphs *sh*, *ch*, and *th*

Have students listen for the consonant digraphs in the words listed on the back of each sound card. Say:

I'm going to say words that have the sound of /sh/, /ch/, or /th/ at the beginning or the end of them. First, I want you to tell me whether you hear /sh/, /ch/, or /th/. Second, tell me the two letters that have that sound. Listen: shed (/sh/, s-h), moth (/th/, t-h), thick (/th/, t-h), chin (/ch/, c-h), fish (/sh/, s-h), three (/th/, t-h), bench (/ch/, c-h), truth (/th/, t-h).

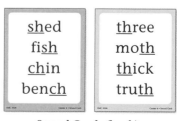

Sound Cards (back)

Consonant Digraphs Review *(continued)*

Leading the Center Activities

1. Read, Discriminate, and Identify ....

Give each student Mat A and a set of task cards. Point out the three rows of digraphs on the mat and review the sound of each digraph: /ch/, /sh/, /th/. Then show the card with the picture of a chain on it and say:

*The picture on this card is a chain. Say the word after me: **chain**. (chain) Do you hear /ch/, /sh/, or /th/ in the word **chain**? (/ch/) Which letters on the mat say /ch/? (c-h) Place the card in the row for **c-h**.*

Repeat this process with the pictures on the remaining cards. Then have students say the word for each picture and tell where they hear the particular digraph sound—at the beginning or at the end of the word. (beginning: chain, chimney, shark, shoe, thousand; end: leash, mouth, sandwich, tooth)

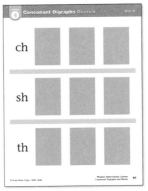

Mat A

2. Read and Understand ....

Have students turn over their mats. Distribute the task cards for Mat B. Then say:

*We're going to form words that name the pictures on this mat. Each word begins or ends with /ch/, /sh/, or /th/. Look at the picture in row 1. It shows a bolt of cloth. Do you hear /ch/, /sh/, or /th/ in the word **cloth**? (/th/) Do you hear /th/ at the beginning of the word **cloth** or at the end? (end) Now look at the letters on your cards. Which letters say /th/? (t-h) Place a **t-h** card after the letters **c-l-o**. Now let's blend the sounds and read the word: /kl/ /ŏ/ /th/ **cloth**.*

Repeat this process with the pictures in the remaining rows. If your students are capable, have them tell you the names of the pictures rather than you saying them. (beach, chimp, brush, thirteen, sheep)

Mat B

3. Practice the Skill ....

Distribute the Practice It! activity (page 107) to students. Read the directions aloud. Then say:

*Look at the first picture. It is a shovel. Do you hear /ch/, /sh/, or /th/ in the word **shovel**? (/sh/) Which letters say /sh/? (s-h) Now circle **s-h** below the picture.*

Repeat this process with the remaining pictures. If your students are capable, have them tell you the names of the pictures rather than you saying them. (couch, booth, shorts, thumb, trash, branch, chalk, moth)

Page 107

Apply and Assess

After the lesson, distribute the Read It! activity (page 108) to students and read the directions aloud. Have students complete the activity independently. Then listen to them read the sentences. Use the results as an informal assessment of students' skill mastery.

Page 108

ch

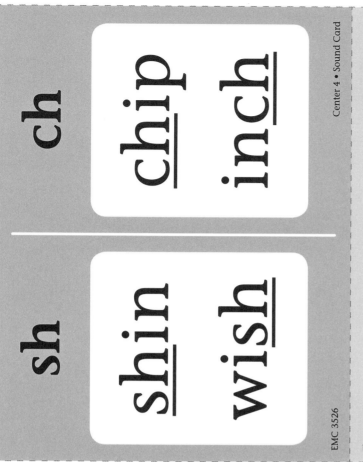

chi**p**

in**ch**

sh

shin

wi**sh**

EMC 3526

th

thank

ma**th**

EMC 3526

Answer Keys

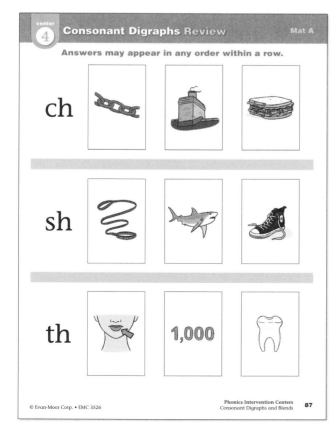

center 4 — **Consonant Digraphs Review** — Mat A

Answers may appear in any order within a row.

ch

sh

th

Phonics Intervention Centers
Consonant Digraphs and Blends — **87**

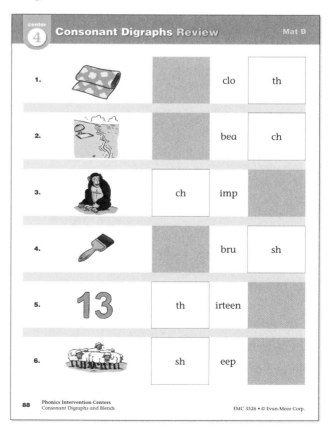

center 4 — **Consonant Digraphs Review** — Mat B

1. clo | th
2. bea | ch
3. ch | imp
4. bru | sh
5. 13 | th | irteen
6. sh | eep

88 Phonics Intervention Centers
Consonant Digraphs and Blends

three
moth
thick
truth

Center 4 • Sound Card

shed
fish
chin
bench

Center 4 • Sound Card

Answer Keys

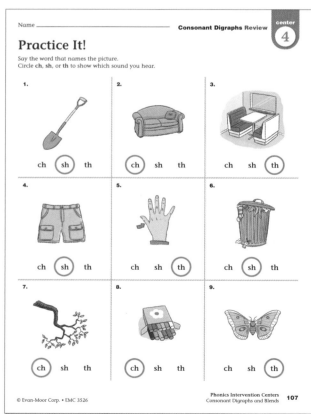

Name _____

Practice It!

Say the word that names the picture.
Circle **ch**, **sh**, or **th** to show which sound you hear.

Consonant Digraphs **Review**

center 4

1. ch (sh) th
2. (ch) sh th
3. ch sh (th)
4. ch (sh) th
5. ch sh (th)
6. ch (sh) th
7. (ch) sh th
8. (ch) sh th
9. ch sh (th)

© Evan-Moor Corp. • EMC 3526

Phonics Intervention Centers
Consonant Digraphs and Blends   **107**

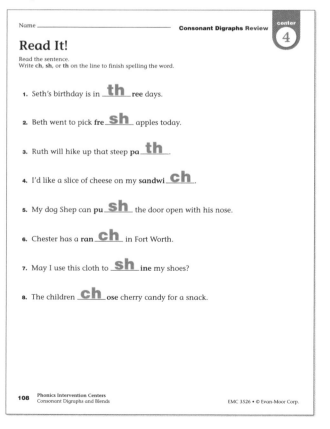

Name _____

Read It!

Read the sentence.
Write **ch**, **sh**, or **th** on the line to finish spelling the word.

Consonant Digraphs **Review**

center 4

1. Seth's birthday is in __**th**__ ree days.

2. Beth went to pick **fre** __**sh**__ apples today.

3. Ruth will hike up that steep **pa** __**th**__ .

4. I'd like a slice of cheese on my **sandwi** __**ch**__ .

5. My dog Shep can **pu** __**sh**__ the door open with his nose.

6. Chester has a **ran** __**ch**__ in Fort Worth.

7. May I use this cloth to __**sh**__ ine my shoes?

8. The children __**ch**__ ose cherry candy for a snack.

108 Phonics Intervention Centers
Consonant Digraphs and Blends

EMC 3526 • © Evan-Moor Corp.

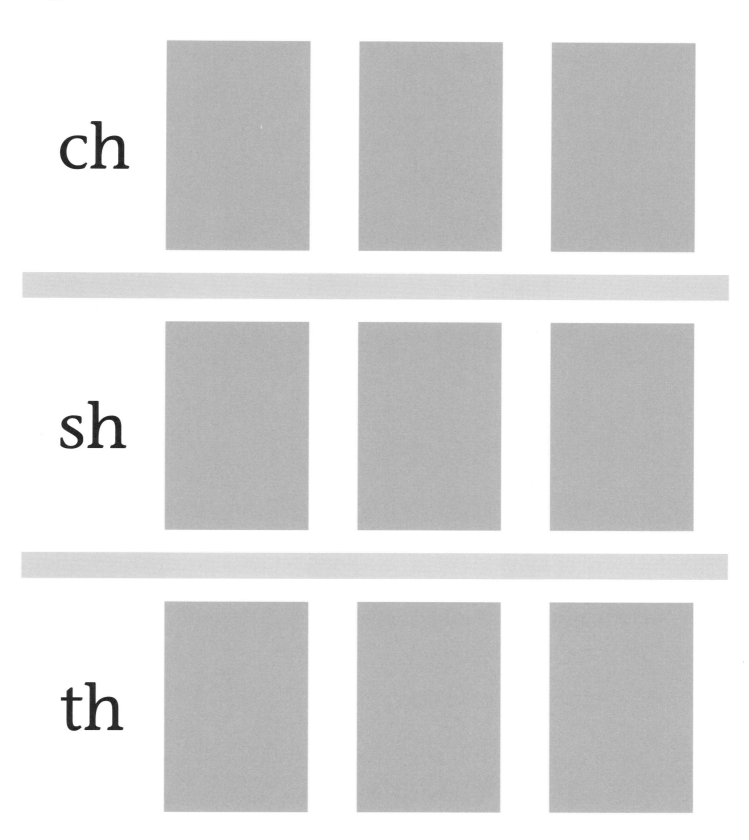

ch

sh

th

1.   clo

2.   bea

3.   imp

4.   bru

5. **13**   irteen

6.   eep

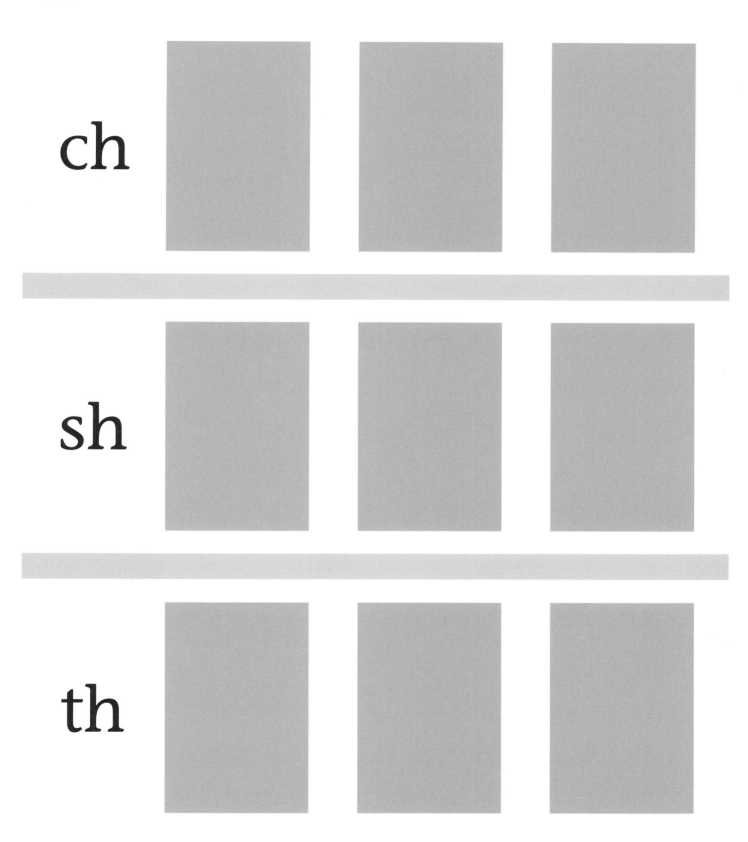

ch

sh

th

1.

2.

3.

4.

5.

6.

clo

bea

imp

bru

irteen

eep

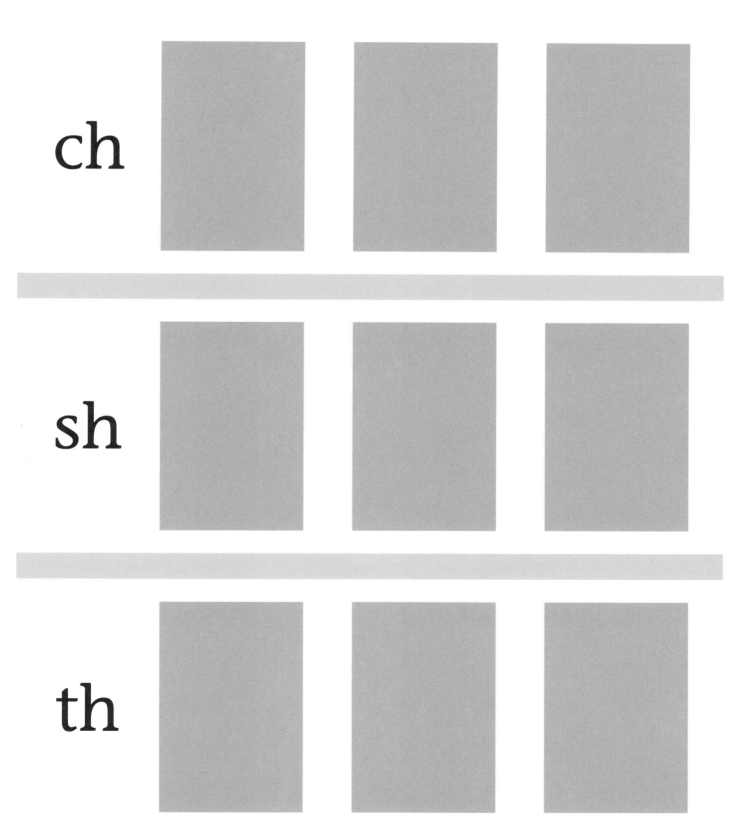

ch

sh

th

1.   clo

2.   bea

3.   imp

4.   bru

5.   irteen

6.   eep

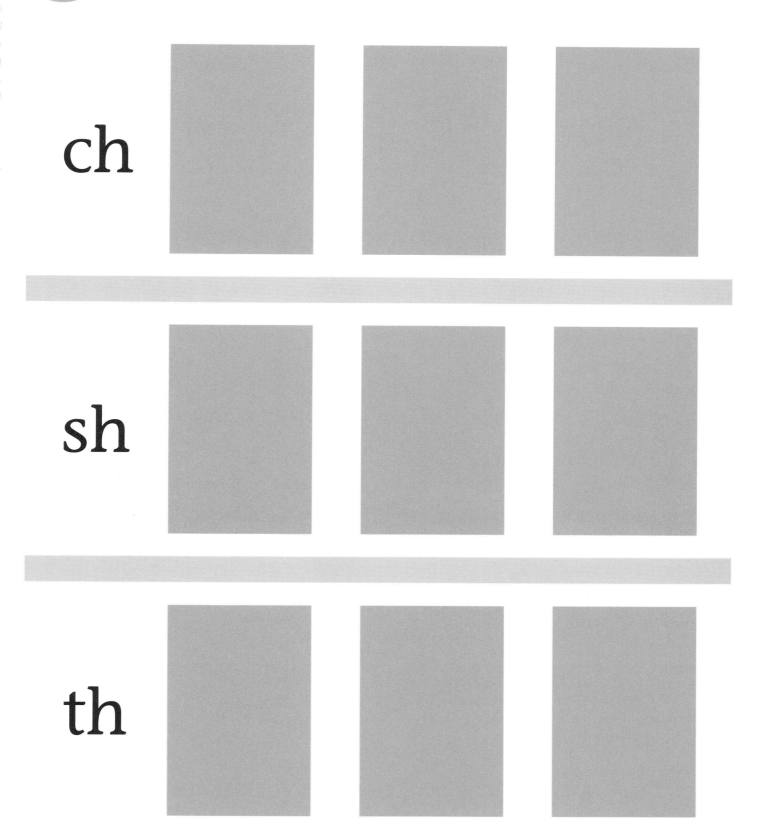

ch

sh

th

1. clo

2. bea

3. imp

4. bru

5. **13** irteen

6. eep

Phonics Intervention Centers
Consonant Digraphs and Blends

EMC 3526 • © Evan-Moor Corp.

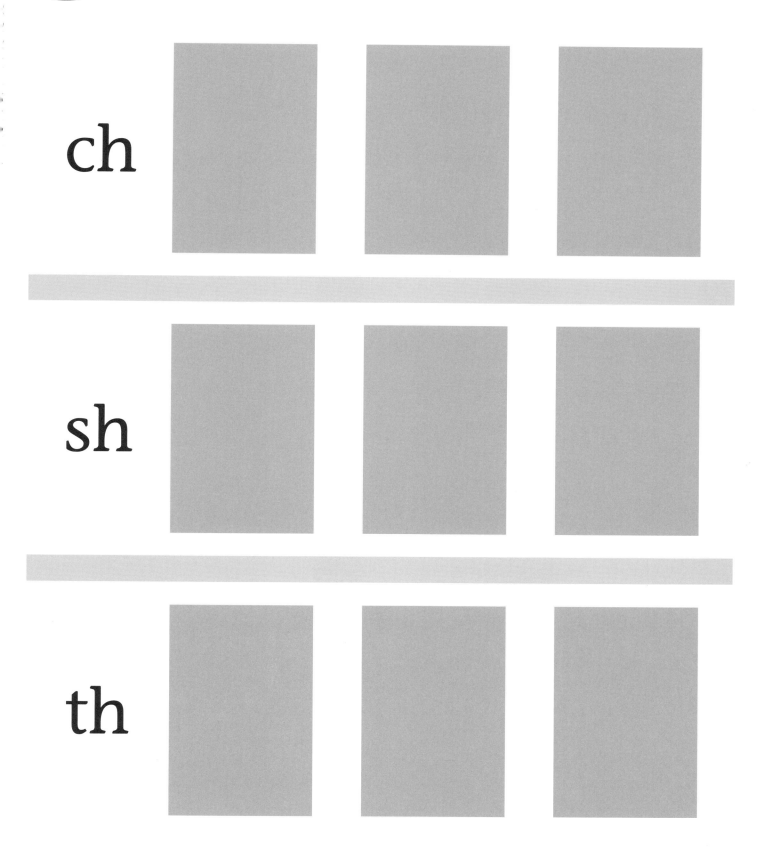

ch

sh

th

1. clo

2. bea

3. imp

4. bru

5. 13 irteen

6. eep

ch

sh

th

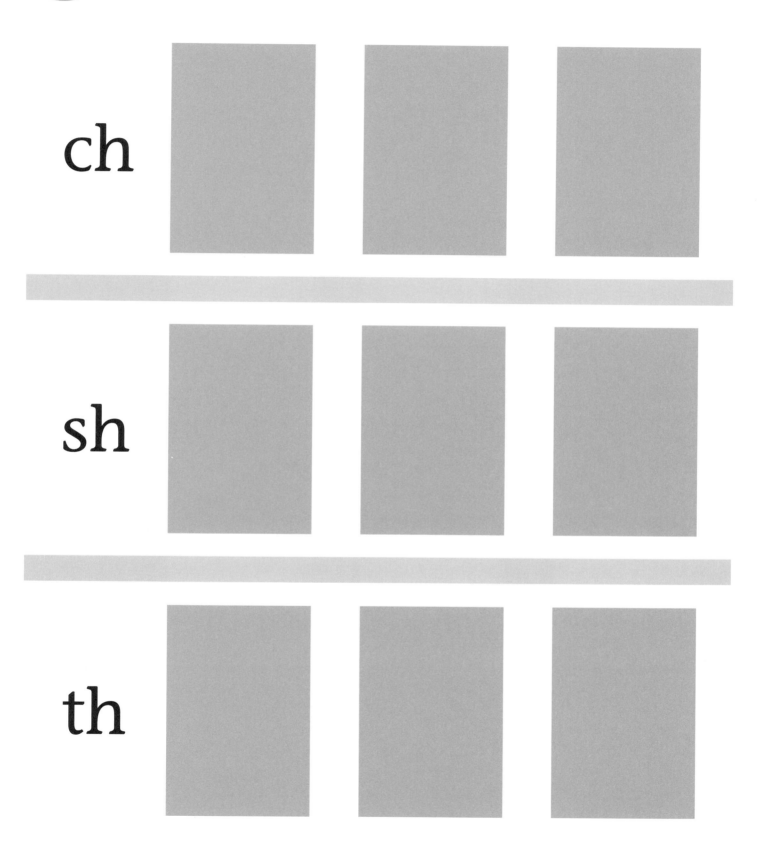

1. clo

2. bea

3. imp

4. bru

5. **13** irteen

6. eep

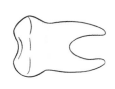

Student 2

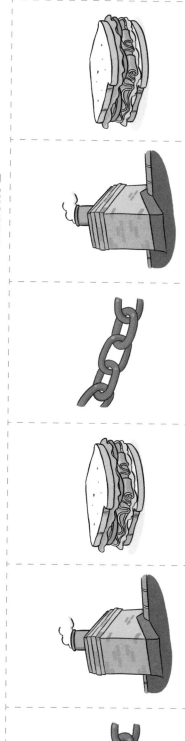

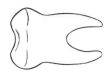

Student 1

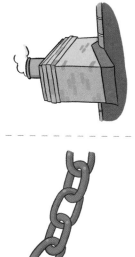

Phonics Intervention Centers
Consonant Digraphs and Blends

Student 2

EMC 3526
Center 4 • Mat A

Student 2

EMC 3526
Center 4 • Mat A

Student 2

EMC 3526
Center 4 • Mat A

Student 2

EMC 3526
Center 4 • Mat A

Student 2

EMC 3526
Center 4 • Mat A

Student 2

EMC 3526
Center 4 • Mat A

Student 1

EMC 3526
Center 4 • Mat A

Student 1

EMC 3526
Center 4 • Mat A

Student 1

EMC 3526
Center 4 • Mat A

Student 1

EMC 3526
Center 4 • Mat A

Student 1

EMC 3526
Center 4 • Mat A

Student 1

EMC 3526
Center 4 • Mat A

Student 4

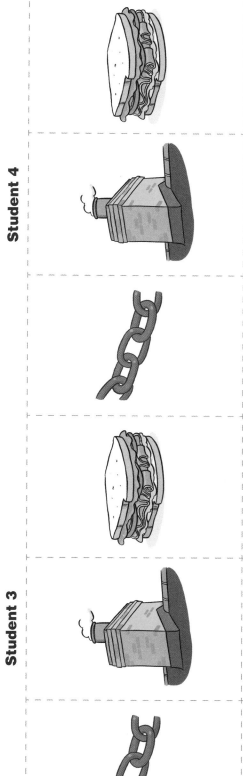

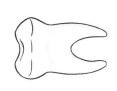

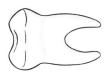

Student 3

Student 4

EMC 3526
Center 4 • Mat A

Student 4

EMC 3526
Center 4 • Mat A

Student 4

EMC 3526
Center 4 • Mat A

Student 4

EMC 3526
Center 4 • Mat A

Student 4

EMC 3526
Center 4 • Mat A

Student 3

EMC 3526
Center 4 • Mat A

Student 4

EMC 3526
Center 4 • Mat A

Student 3

EMC 3526
Center 4 • Mat A

Student 3

EMC 3526
Center 4 • Mat A

Student 3

EMC 3526
Center 4 • Mat A

Student 3

EMC 3526
Center 4 • Mat A

Student 3

EMC 3526
Center 4 • Mat A

Student 6

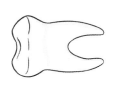

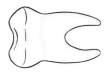

Student 5

Student 6

EMC 3526
Center 4 • Mat A

Student 6

EMC 3526
Center 4 • Mat A

Student 6

EMC 3526
Center 4 • Mat A

Student 6

EMC 3526
Center 4 • Mat A

Student 6

EMC 3526
Center 4 • Mat A

Student 6

EMC 3526
Center 4 • Mat A

Student 6

EMC 3526
Center 4 • Mat A

Student 6

EMC 3526
Center 4 • Mat A

Student 5

EMC 3526
Center 4 • Mat A

Student 5

EMC 3526
Center 4 • Mat A

Student 5

EMC 3526
Center 4 • Mat A

Student 5

EMC 3526
Center 4 • Mat A

Student 5

EMC 3526
Center 4 • Mat A

Student 5

EMC 3526
Center 4 • Mat A

Student 5

EMC 3526
Center 4 • Mat A

Student 5

EMC 3526
Center 4 • Mat A

Student 6	Student 5	Student 4	Student 3	Student 2	Student 1
ch	ch	ch	ch	ch	ch
ch	ch	ch	ch	ch	ch
sh	sh	sh	sh	sh	sh
sh	sh	sh	sh	sh	sh
th	th	th	th	th	th
th	th	th	th	th	th

Student 6 EMC 3526 Center 4 • Mat B	**Student 5** EMC 3526 Center 4 • Mat B
Student 6 EMC 3526 Center 4 • Mat B	**Student 5** EMC 3526 Center 4 • Mat B
Student 6 EMC 3526 Center 4 • Mat B	**Student 5** EMC 3526 Center 4 • Mat B
Student 6 EMC 3526 Center 4 • Mat B	**Student 5** EMC 3526 Center 4 • Mat B
Student 6 EMC 3526 Center 4 • Mat B	**Student 5** EMC 3526 Center 4 • Mat B
Student 6 EMC 3526 Center 4 • Mat B	**Student 5** EMC 3526 Center 4 • Mat B

Student 4 EMC 3526 Center 4 • Mat B	**Student 3** EMC 3526 Center 4 • Mat B
Student 4 EMC 3526 Center 4 • Mat B	**Student 3** EMC 3526 Center 4 • Mat B
Student 4 EMC 3526 Center 4 • Mat B	**Student 3** EMC 3526 Center 4 • Mat B
Student 4 EMC 3526 Center 4 • Mat B	**Student 3** EMC 3526 Center 4 • Mat B
Student 4 EMC 3526 Center 4 • Mat B	**Student 3** EMC 3526 Center 4 • Mat B
Student 4 EMC 3526 Center 4 • Mat B	**Student 3** EMC 3526 Center 4 • Mat B

Student 2 EMC 3526 Center 4 • Mat B	**Student 1** EMC 3526 Center 4 • Mat B
Student 2 EMC 3526 Center 4 • Mat B	**Student 1** EMC 3526 Center 4 • Mat B
Student 2 EMC 3526 Center 4 • Mat B	**Student 1** EMC 3526 Center 4 • Mat B
Student 2 EMC 3526 Center 4 • Mat B	**Student 1** EMC 3526 Center 4 • Mat B
Student 2 EMC 3526 Center 4 • Mat B	**Student 1** EMC 3526 Center 4 • Mat B
Student 2 EMC 3526 Center 4 • Mat B	**Student 1** EMC 3526 Center 4 • Mat B

Practice It!

Say the word that names the picture.
Circle **ch**, **sh**, or **th** to show which sound you hear.

1.

ch   sh   th

2.

ch   sh   th

3.

ch   sh   th

4.

ch   sh   th

5.

ch   sh   th

6.

ch   sh   th

7.

ch   sh   th

8.

ch   sh   th

9.

ch   sh   th

Read It!

Read the sentence.
Write **ch**, **sh**, or **th** on the line to finish spelling the word.

1. Seth's birthday is in _____ **ree** days.

2. Beth went to pick **fre** _____ apples today.

3. Ruth will hike up that steep **pa** _____.

4. I'd like a slice of cheese on my **sandwi** _____.

5. My dog Shep can **pu** _____ the door open with his nose.

6. Chester has a **ran** _____ in Fort Worth.

7. May I use this cloth to _____ **ine** my shoes?

8. The children _____ **ose** cherry candy for a snack.

Consonant + r Blends

For the Teacher

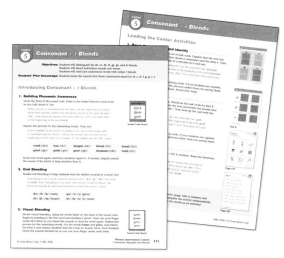

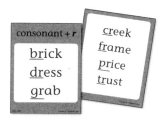

Lesson Plan

Sound Cards

Answer Keys

For the Student

front (Mat A)

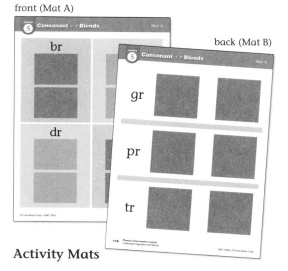

back (Mat B)

Activity Mats

Task Cards

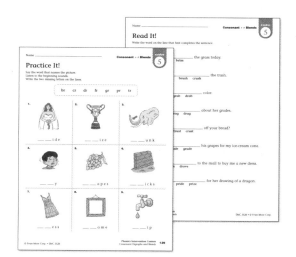

Practice and Assessment Activities

Consonant + r Blends

Objectives: Students will distinguish the *br*, *cr*, *dr*, *fr*, *gr*, *pr*, and *tr* blends.
Students will blend individual sounds into words.
Students will read and understand words with initial *r* blends.

Students' Prior Knowledge: Students know the sounds that these consonants stand for: *b, c, d, f, g, p, r, t.*

Introducing Consonant + *r* Blends

1. Building Phonemic Awareness

Show the front of the sound card. Point to the initial blend in each word as you talk about it. Say:

*When you see a consonant and the letter r at the beginning of a word, blend their sounds. Listen to me blend the sounds of the letters b and r: /br/. Now blend the sounds of b and r with me. (/br/) You hear /br/ at the beginning of the word **brick**.*

consonant + *r*

brick
dress
grab

Sound Card (front)

Repeat this process for the remaining words. Then say:

*Listen carefully to the words I'm going to say. Each word begins with a consonant and the letter r. Tell me the sounds that you hear at the beginning of each word. For example, if I say **truck**, you say /tr/. Listen:*

crush (/kr/)	**tray** (/tr/)	**dragon** (/dr/)	**friend** (/fr/)	**bread** (/br/)
great (/gr/)	**pride** (/pr/)	**grow** (/gr/)	**drummer** (/dr/)	**truth** (/tr/)

Read each word again and have students repeat it. If needed, slightly stretch the sound of the blend to help students hear it.

2. Oral Blending

Model oral blending to help students hear the distinct sounds in a word. Say:

*I am going to say a word, sound by sound. Listen: /kr/ /ă/ /sh/. The word is **crash**. Now I am going to say some other words, sound by sound. You blend the sounds for each word and tell me what the word is. Listen:*

/kr/ /ē/ /k/ (creek)	/pr/ /ī/ /s/ (price)
/fr/ /ā/ /m/ (frame)	/tr/ /ŭ/ /s/ /t/ (trust)

3. Visual Blending

Model visual blending, using the words listed on the back of the sound card. Begin by pointing to the first word and reading it aloud. Then run your finger under the letters as you blend the sounds to read the word again. Repeat this process for the remaining words. For the words **frame** and **price**, stop before the final *e* and remind students that the *e* has no sound. Next, have students blend the sounds themselves as you run your finger under each letter.

creek
frame
price
trust

Sound Card (back)

Consonant + r Blends (continued)

Leading the Center Activities

1. Read, Discriminate, and Identify

Give each student Mat A and a set of task cards. Explain that the mat has four sections and that each section shows a consonant and the letter *r*. Then hold up the card with the picture of a bracelet on it and say:

*This card shows a picture of a bracelet. Say the word after me: **bracelet**.*
*(bracelet) What sounds do you hear at the beginning of the word **bracelet**?*
*(/br/) Which letters on the mat say /**br**/? (b-r) Now place this card in the*
***b-r** section of the mat.*

Repeat this process with the remaining cards. If your students are capable, have them tell you the names of the pictures rather than you saying them. (bread, crocodile, crow, dragon, drum, french fries, frog)

2. Read and Understand

Have students turn over their mats. Distribute the task cards for Mat B. Point out the three rows of blends on the mat and review the sounds that each blend stands for: /**gr**/, /**pr**/, /**tr**/. Then hold up the card with the picture of a grill on it and say:

*This card shows a picture of a grill. Say the word after me: **grill**.*
*(grill) What sounds do you hear at the beginning of the word **grill**?*
*(/gr/) Which letters on the mat say /**gr**/? (g-r) Now place this card*
*in the row for **g-r**.*

Repeat this process with the remaining cards. If your students are capable, have them tell you the names of the pictures rather than you saying them. (gray, pretzel, printer, triangle, trunk)

3. Practice the Skill

Distribute the Practice It! activity (page 139) to students. Read the directions aloud. Then say:

Look at the first picture. It is a bride. Say the sounds that you hear at
*the beginning of the word **bride**. (/br/) What letters say /**br**/? (b-r)*
*Write the letters **b-r** on the lines under the picture. Now let's blend*
*the sounds and read the word: /**br**/ /ī/ /d/ **bride**.*

Repeat this process to complete the page.

Apply and Assess

After the lesson, distribute the Read It! activity (page 140) to students and read the directions aloud. Have students complete the activity independently. Then listen to them read the sentences. Use the results as an informal assessment of students' skill mastery.

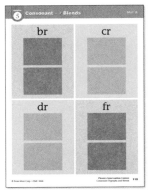

Mat A

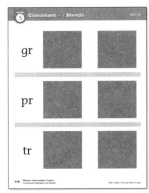

Mat B

Page 139

Page 140

consonant + *r*

<u>br</u>ick

<u>dr</u>ess

<u>gr</u>ab

EMC 3526

Center 5 • Sound Card

Answer Keys

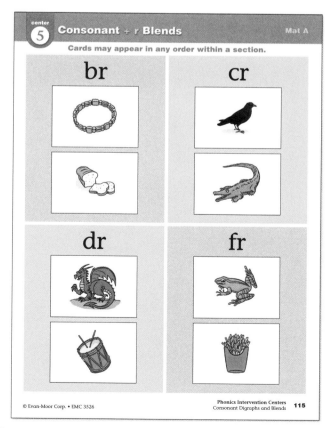

creek
frame
price
trust

Answer Keys

Name _____

Consonant + r Blends

center 5

Practice It!

Say the word that names the picture.
Listen to the beginning sounds.
Write the two missing letters on the lines.

br cr dr fr gr pr tr

1. **b r** ide
2. **p r** ize
3. **t r** unk
4. **c r** y
5. **g r** apes
6. **b r** icks
7. **d r** ess
8. **f r** ame
9. **d r** ip

© Evan-Moor Corp. • EMC 3526

Phonics Intervention Centers
Consonant Digraphs and Blends **139**

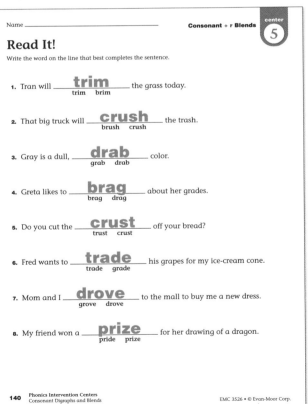

Name _____

Consonant + r Blends

center 5

Read It!

Write the word on the line that best completes the sentence.

1. Tran will _____**trim**_____ the grass today.
   trim brim

2. That big truck will _____**crush**_____ the trash.
   brush crush

3. Gray is a dull, _____**drab**_____ color.
   grab drab

4. Greta likes to _____**brag**_____ about her grades.
   brag drag

5. Do you cut the _____**crust**_____ off your bread?
   trust crust

6. Fred wants to _____**trade**_____ his grapes for my ice-cream cone.
   trade grade

7. Mom and I _____**drove**_____ to the mall to buy me a new dress.
   grove drove

8. My friend won a _____**prize**_____ for her drawing of a dragon.
   pride prize

140 Phonics Intervention Centers
Consonant Digraphs and Blends

EMC 3526 • © Evan-Moor Corp.

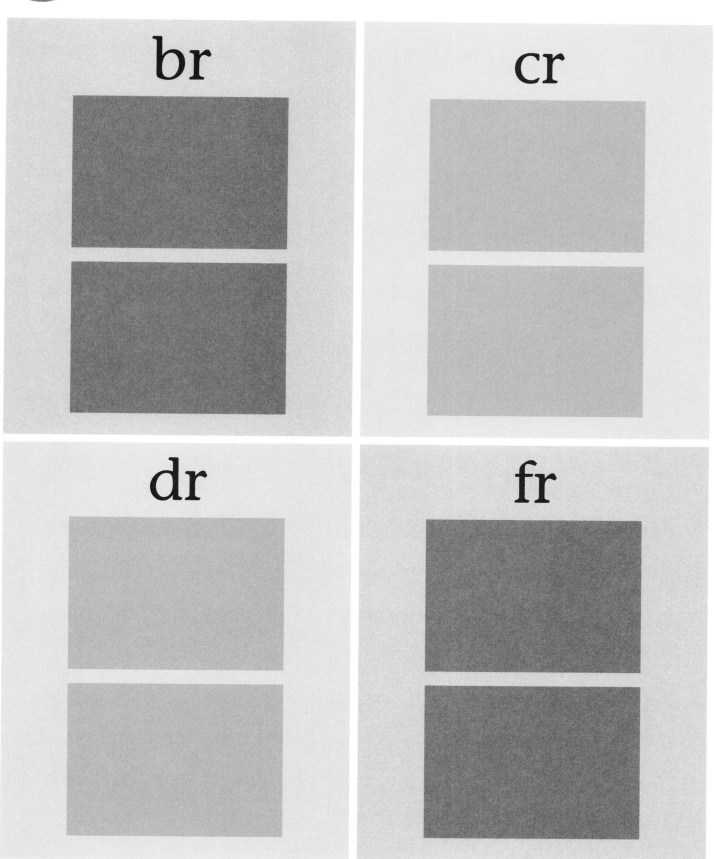

br

cr

dr

fr

gr

pr

tr

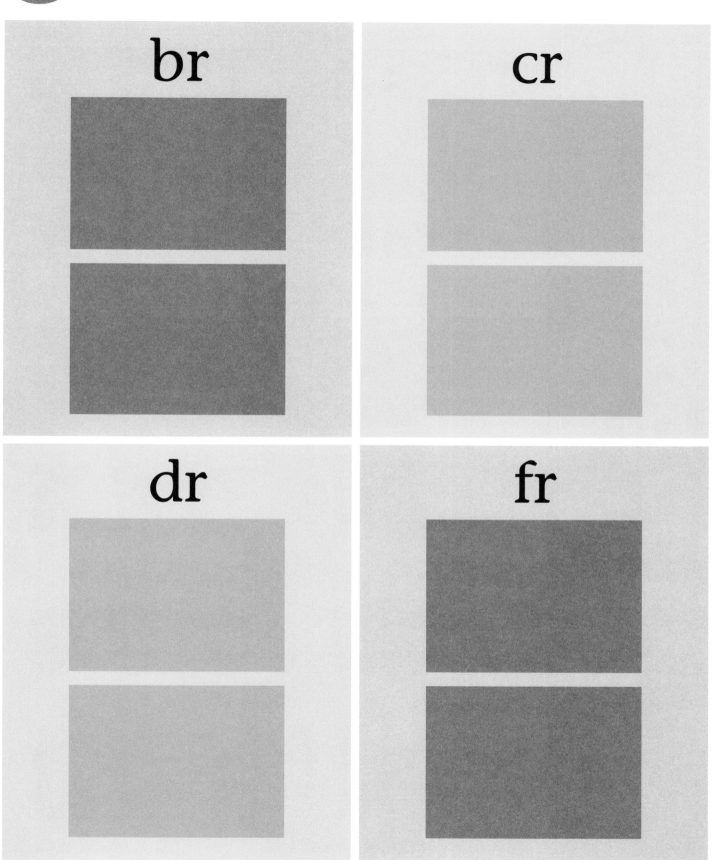

gr

pr

tr

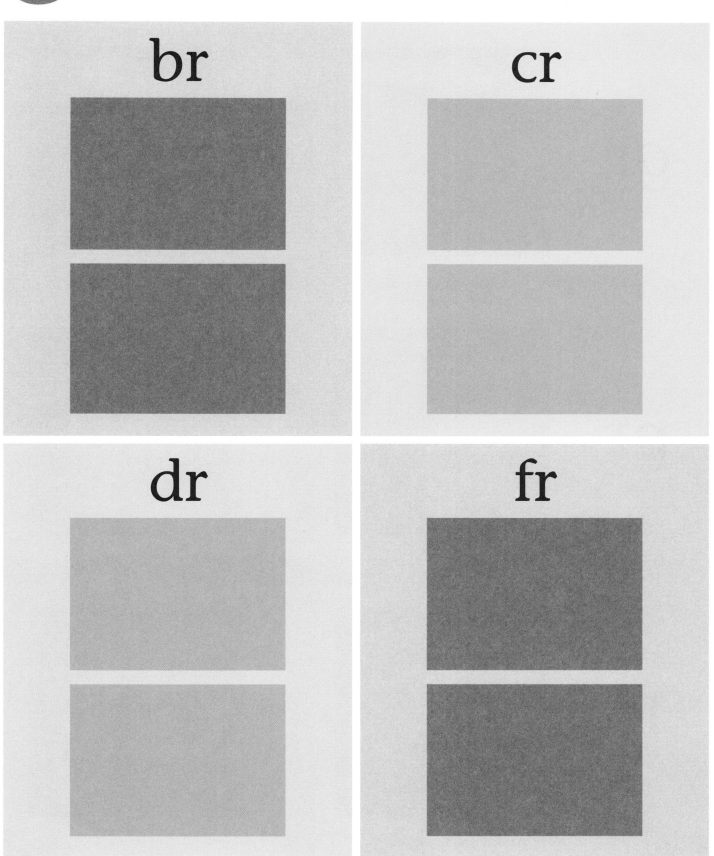

br

cr

dr

fr

gr

pr

tr

Phonics Intervention Centers
Consonant Digraphs and Blends

EMC 3526 • © Evan-Moor Corp.

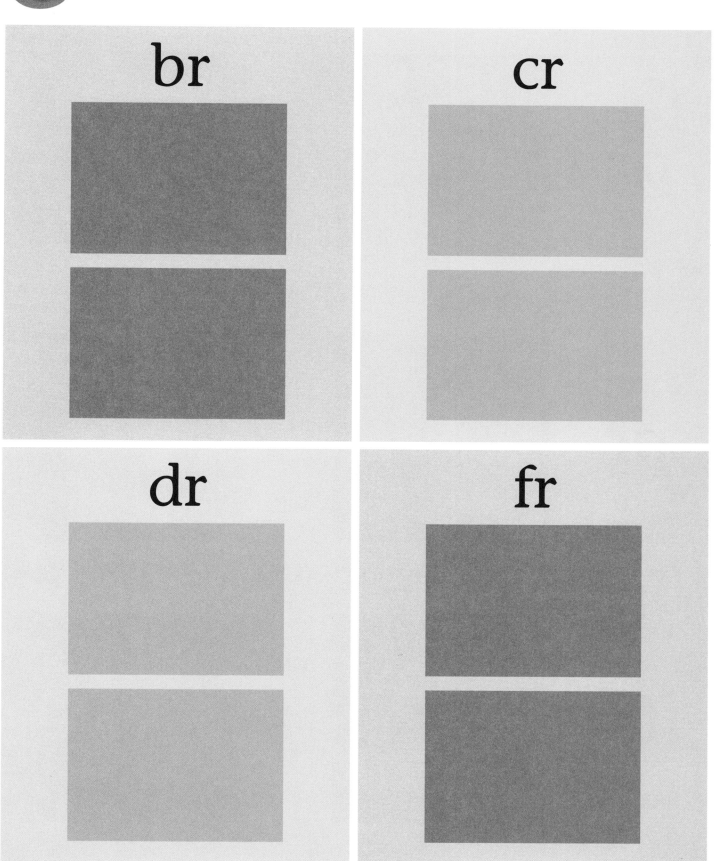

br

cr

dr

fr

gr

pr

tr

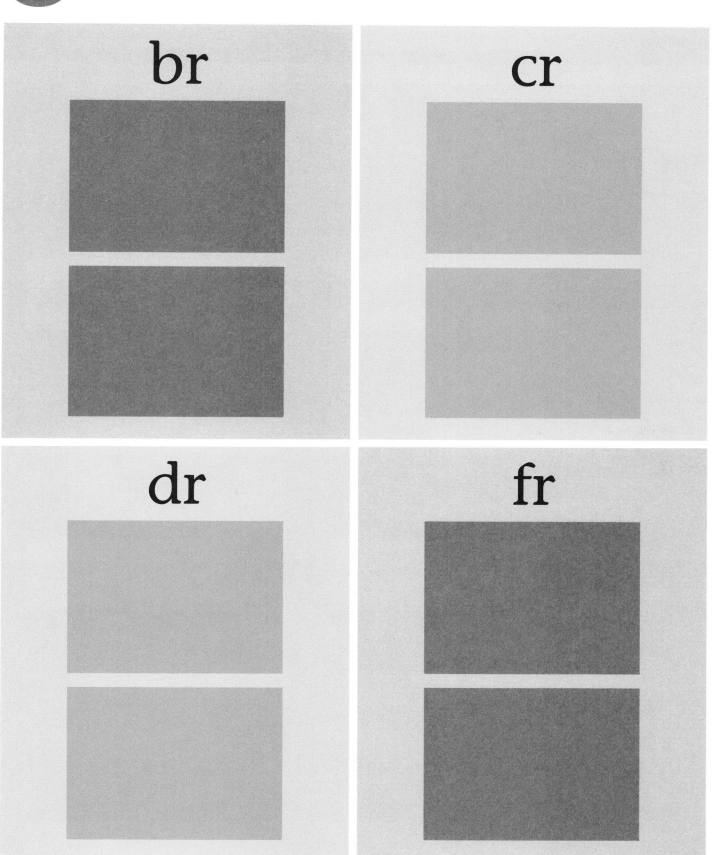

gr

pr

tr

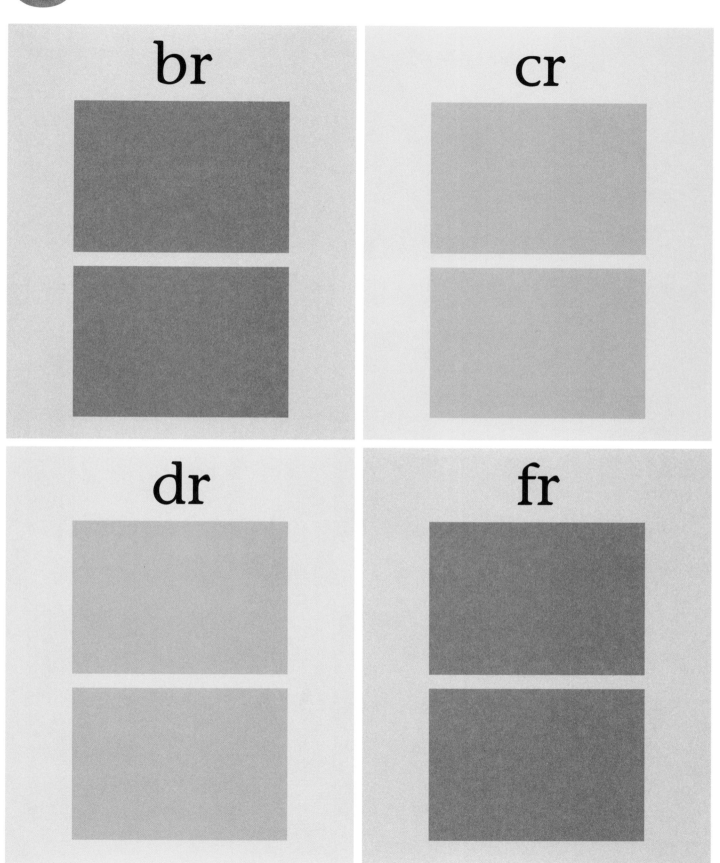

br

cr

dr

fr

gr

pr

tr

Student 2

Student 1

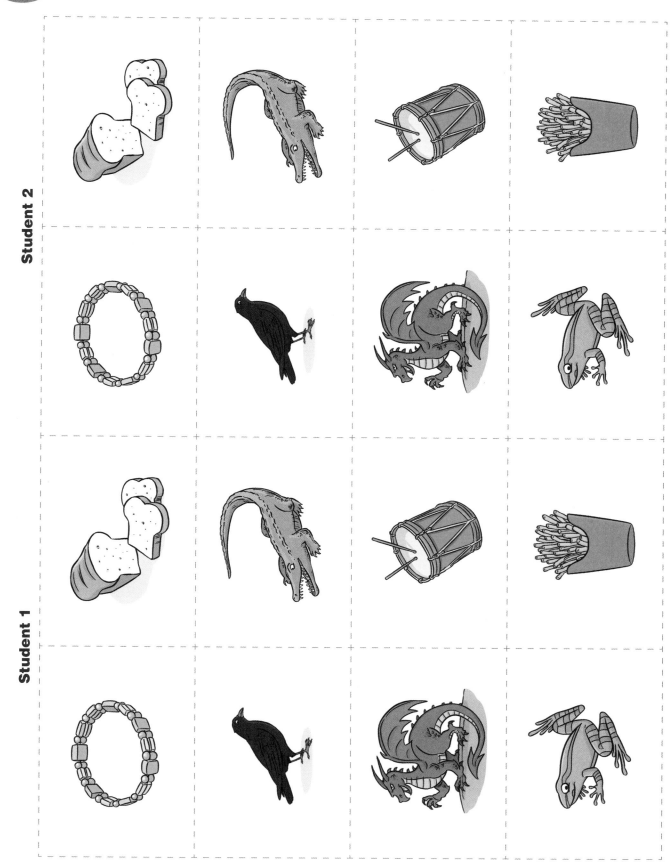

Student 2

EMC 3526 • Center 5 • Mat A

Student 2

EMC 3526 • Center 5 • Mat A

Student 2

EMC 3526 • Center 5 • Mat A

Student 2

EMC 3526 • Center 5 • Mat A

Student 2

EMC 3526 • Center 5 • Mat A

Student 2

EMC 3526 • Center 5 • Mat A

Student 2

EMC 3526 • Center 5 • Mat A

Student 2

EMC 3526 • Center 5 • Mat A

Student 1

EMC 3526 • Center 5 • Mat A

Student 1

EMC 3526 • Center 5 • Mat A

Student 1

EMC 3526 • Center 5 • Mat A

Student 1

EMC 3526 • Center 5 • Mat A

Student 1

EMC 3526 • Center 5 • Mat A

Student 1

EMC 3526 • Center 5 • Mat A

Student 1

EMC 3526 • Center 5 • Mat A

Student 1

EMC 3526 • Center 5 • Mat A

Student 4

Student 3

Student 4

EMC 3526 • Center 5 • Mat A

Student 4

EMC 3526 • Center 5 • Mat A

Student 4

EMC 3526 • Center 5 • Mat A

Student 4

EMC 3526 • Center 5 • Mat A

Student 4

EMC 3526 • Center 5 • Mat A

Student 4

EMC 3526 • Center 5 • Mat A

Student 3

EMC 3526 • Center 5 • Mat A

Student 3

EMC 3526 • Center 5 • Mat A

Student 3

EMC 3526 • Center 5 • Mat A

Student 3

EMC 3526 • Center 5 • Mat A

Student 3

EMC 3526 • Center 5 • Mat A

Student 3

EMC 3526 • Center 5 • Mat A

Student 6

Student 5

Student 6

EMC 3526 • Center 5 • Mat A

Student 6

EMC 3526 • Center 5 • Mat A

Student 6

EMC 3526 • Center 5 • Mat A

Student 6

EMC 3526 • Center 5 • Mat A

Student 6

EMC 3526 • Center 5 • Mat A

Student 6

EMC 3526 • Center 5 • Mat A

Student 6

EMC 3526 • Center 5 • Mat A

Student 6

EMC 3526 • Center 5 • Mat A

Student 5

EMC 3526 • Center 5 • Mat A

Student 5

EMC 3526 • Center 5 • Mat A

Student 5

EMC 3526 • Center 5 • Mat A

Student 5

EMC 3526 • Center 5 • Mat A

Student 5

EMC 3526 • Center 5 • Mat A

Student 5

EMC 3526 • Center 5 • Mat A

Student 5

EMC 3526 • Center 5 • Mat A

Student 5

EMC 3526 • Center 5 • Mat A

Student 2

Student 1

Student 2

Student 2

Student 2

Student 2

Student 2

Student 1

Student 2

Student 1

Student 1

Student 1

Student 1

Student 1

Student 4

 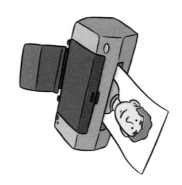 

Student 3

Student 4

EMC 3526 • Center 5 • Mat B

Student 4

EMC 3526 • Center 5 • Mat B

Student 4

EMC 3526 • Center 5 • Mat B

Student 4

EMC 3526 • Center 5 • Mat B

Student 4

EMC 3526 • Center 5 • Mat B

Student 3

EMC 3526 • Center 5 • Mat B

Student 4

EMC 3526 • Center 5 • Mat B

Student 3

EMC 3526 • Center 5 • Mat B

Student 3

EMC 3526 • Center 5 • Mat B

Student 3

EMC 3526 • Center 5 • Mat B

Student 3

EMC 3526 • Center 5 • Mat B

Student 3

EMC 3526 • Center 5 • Mat B

Student 6

Student 5

Student 6

EMC 3526 • Center 5 • Mat B

Student 6

EMC 3526 • Center 5 • Mat B

Student 6

EMC 3526 • Center 5 • Mat B

Student 6

EMC 3526 • Center 5 • Mat B

Student 6

EMC 3526 • Center 5 • Mat B

Student 6

EMC 3526 • Center 5 • Mat B

Student 5

EMC 3526 • Center 5 • Mat B

Student 5

EMC 3526 • Center 5 • Mat B

Student 5

EMC 3526 • Center 5 • Mat B

Student 5

EMC 3526 • Center 5 • Mat B

Student 5

EMC 3526 • Center 5 • Mat B

Student 5

EMC 3526 • Center 5 • Mat B

Practice It!

Say the word that names the picture.
Listen to the beginning sounds.
Write the two missing letters on the lines.

br   cr   dr   fr   gr   pr   tr

1.

___ ___ i d e

2.

___ ___ i z e

3.

___ ___ u n k

4.

___ ___ y

5.

___ ___ a p e s

6.

___ ___ i c k s

7.

___ ___ e s s

8.

___ ___ a m e

9.

___ ___ i p

Name _____

Read It!

Write the word on the line that best completes the sentence.

1. Tran will _____ the grass today.
   trim   brim

2. That big truck will _____ the trash.
   brush   crush

3. Gray is a dull, _____ color.
   grab   drab

4. Greta likes to _____ about her grades.
   brag   drag

5. Do you cut the _____ off your bread?
   trust   crust

6. Fred wants to _____ his grapes for my ice-cream cone.
   trade   grade

7. Mom and I _____ to the mall to buy me a new dress.
   grove   drove

8. My friend won a _____ for her drawing of a dragon.
   pride   prize

Consonant + l Blends

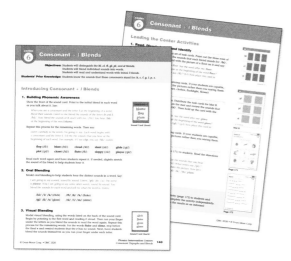

Lesson Plan

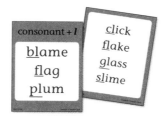

Sound Cards

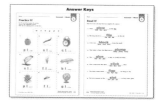

Answer Keys

front (Mat A)

back (Mat B)

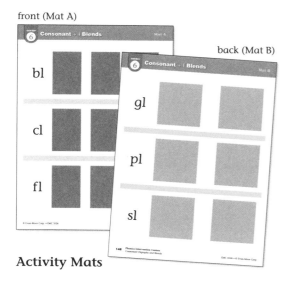

Activity Mats

Task Cards

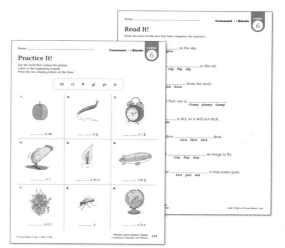

Practice and Assessment Activities

Consonant + l Blends

Objectives: Students will distinguish the *bl*, *cl*, *fl*, *gl*, *pl*, and *sl* blends.
Students will blend individual sounds into words.
Students will read and understand words with initial *l* blends.

Students' Prior Knowledge: Students know the sounds that these consonants stand for: *b, c, f, g, l, p, s*.

Introducing Consonant + *l* Blends

1. Building Phonemic Awareness

Show the front of the sound card. Point to the initial blend in each word as you talk about it. Say:

Sound Card (front)

*When you see a consonant and the letter **l** at the beginning of a word, blend their sounds. Listen to me blend the sounds of the letters **b** and **l**: /bl/. Now blend the sounds of **b** and **l** with me. (/bl/) You hear /**bl**/ at the beginning of the word **blame**.*

Repeat this process for the remaining words. Then say:

*Listen carefully to the words I'm going to say. Each word begins with a consonant and the letter **l**. Tell me the sounds that you hear at the beginning of each word. For example, if I say **clip**, you say /kl/. Listen:*

flop (/fl/)	**blast** (/bl/)	**cloud** (/kl/)	**slant** (/sl/)	**glide** (/gl/)
plot (/pl/)	**closet** (/kl/)	**flute** (/fl/)	**sloppy** (/sl/)	**player** (/pl/)

Read each word again and have students repeat it. If needed, slightly stretch the sound of the blend to help students hear it.

2. Oral Blending

Model oral blending to help students hear the distinct sounds in a word. Say:

*I am going to say a word, sound by sound. Listen: /pl/ /ē/ /z/. The word is **please**. Now I am going to say some other words, sound by sound. You blend the sounds for each word and tell me what the word is. Listen:*

/kl/ /ĭ/ /k/ (click)	/fl/ /ā/ /k/ (flake)
/gl/ /ă/ /s/ (glass)	/sl/ /ī/ /m/ (slime)

3. Visual Blending

Model visual blending, using the words listed on the back of the sound card. Begin by pointing to the first word and reading it aloud. Then run your finger under the letters as you blend the sounds to read the word again. Repeat this process for the remaining words. For the words **flake** and **slime**, stop before the final *e* and remind students that the *e* has no sound. Next, have students blend the sounds themselves as you run your finger under each letter.

Sound Card (back)

Consonant + l Blends (continued)

Leading the Center Activities

1. Read, Discriminate, and Identify ....

Give each student Mat A and a set of task cards. Point out the three rows of blends on the mat and review the sounds that each blend stands for: **/bl/**, **/kl/**, **/fl/**. Then hold up the card with the picture of a floor on it and say:

This card shows a picture of a floor. Say the word after me: **floor**. (floor) *What sounds do you hear at the beginning of the word* **floor**? (/fl/) *Which letters on the mat say /fl/?* (f-l) *Now place this card in the row for f-l.*

Repeat this process with the remaining cards. If your students are capable, have them tell you the names of the pictures rather than you saying them. (blanket, blind, blouse, clock, closet, clothes, flashlight, flower)

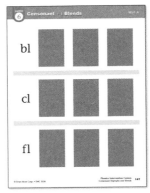

Mat A

2. Read and Understand ....

Have students turn over their mats. Distribute the task cards for Mat B. Point out the three rows of blends on the mat and review the sounds that each blend stands for: **/gl/**, **/pl/**, **/sl/**. Then hold up the card with the picture of a glove on it and say:

This card shows a picture of a glove. Say the word after me: **glove**. (glove) *What sounds do you hear at the beginning of the word* **glove**? (/gl/) *Which letters on the mat say /gl/?* (g-l) *Now place this card in the row for g-l.*

Repeat this process with the remaining cards. If your students are capable, have them tell you the names of the pictures rather than you saying them. (glass, planet, plug, sleeve, slug)

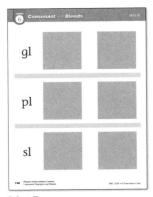

Mat B

3. Practice the Skill ....

Distribute the Practice It! activity (page 171) to students. Read the directions aloud. Then say:

Look at the first picture. It is a plum. Say the sounds that you hear at the beginning of the word **plum**. (/pl/) *What letters say /pl/?* (p-l) *Write the letters* **p-l** *on the lines under the picture. Now let's blend the sounds and read the word: /pl/ /ŭ/ /m/* **plum**.

Repeat this process to complete the page.

Page 171

Apply and Assess

After the lesson, distribute the Read It! activity (page 172) to students and read the directions aloud. Have students complete the activity independently. Then listen to them read the sentences. Use the results as an informal assessment of students' skill mastery.

Page 172

consonant + *l*

blame
flag
plum

EMC 3526

Center 6 • Sound Card

Answer Keys

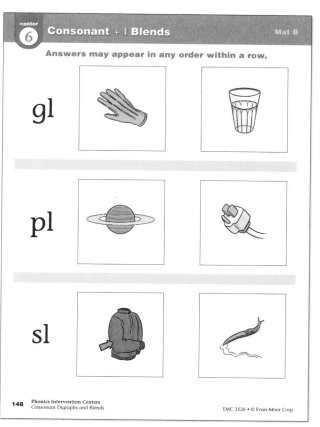

click
flake
glass
slime

EMC 3526

Center 6 • Sound Card

Answer Keys

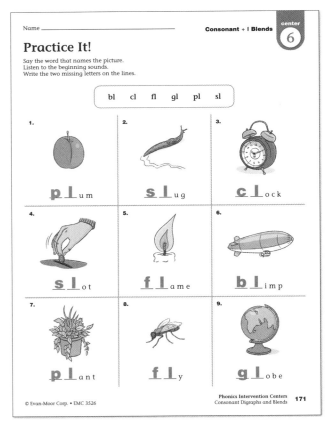

Name _____

Consonant + l Blends

center 6

Practice It!

Say the word that names the picture.
Listen to the beginning sounds.
Write the two missing letters on the lines.

| bl | cl | fl | gl | pl | sl |

1. **p l** um

2. **s l** ug

3. **c l** ock

4. **s l** ot

5. **f l** ame

6. **b l** imp

7. **p l** ant

8. **f l** y

9. **g l** obe

© Evan-Moor Corp. • EMC 3526

Phonics Intervention Centers
Consonant Digraphs and Blends **171**

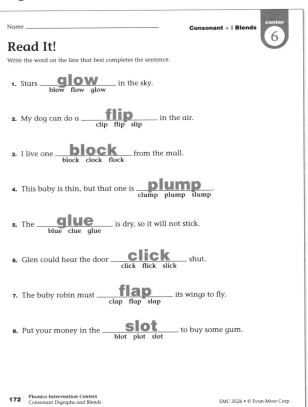

Name _____

Consonant + l Blends

center 6

Read It!

Write the word on the line that best completes the sentence.

1. Stars **glow** in the sky.
   blow flow glow

2. My dog can do a **flip** in the air.
   clip flip slip

3. I live one **block** from the mall.
   block clock flock

4. This baby is thin, but that one is **plump**.
   clump plump slump

5. The **glue** is dry, so it will not stick.
   blue clue glue

6. Glen could hear the door **click** shut.
   click flick slick

7. The baby robin must **flap** its wings to fly.
   clap flap slap

8. Put your money in the **slot** to buy some gum.
   blot plot slot

172 Phonics Intervention Centers
Consonant Digraphs and Blends

EMC 3526 • © Evan-Moor Corp.

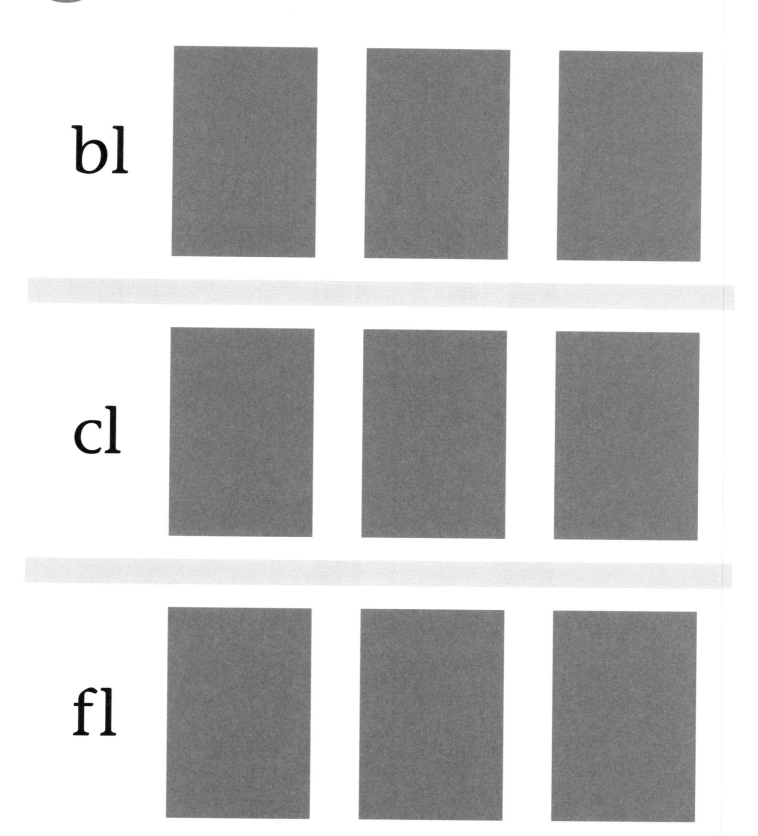

bl

cl

fl

gl

pl

sl

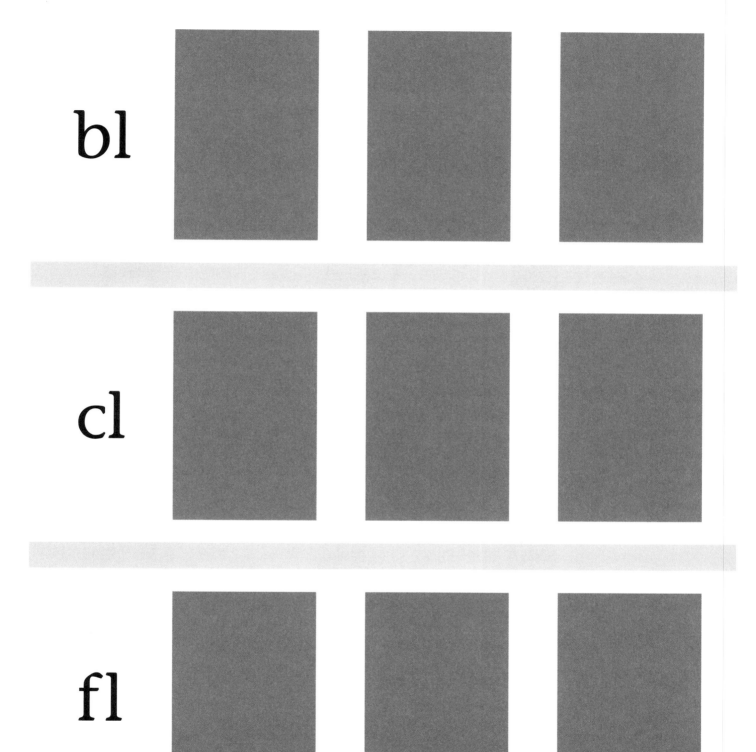

bl

cl

fl

gl

pl

sl

bl

cl

fl

gl

pl

sl

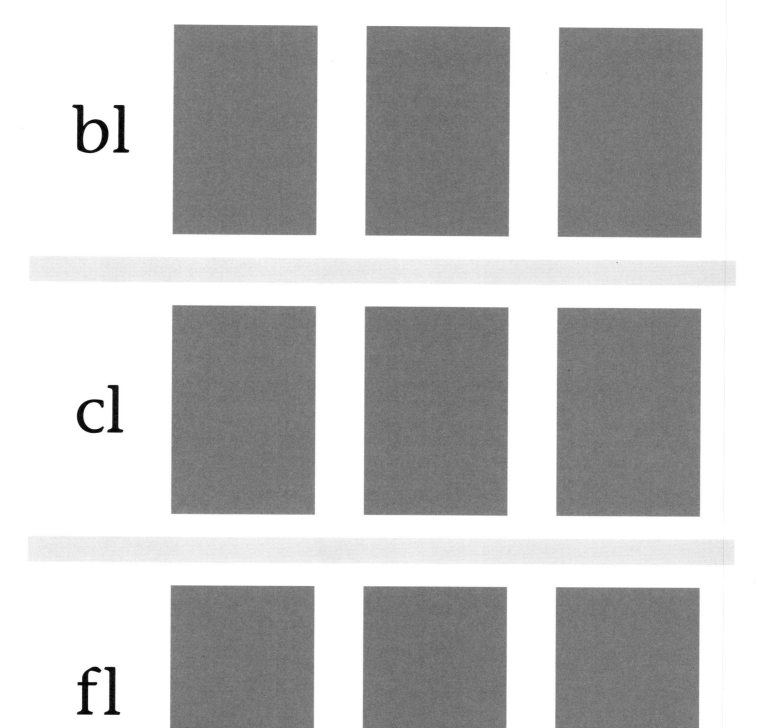

bl

cl

fl

center 6 Consonant + l Blends

Mat B

bl

cl

fl

gl

pl

sl

bl

cl

fl

gl

pl

sl

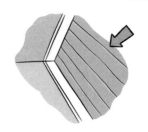

Student 2

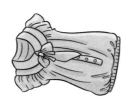

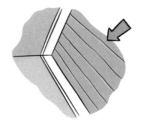

Student 1

Student 2

EMC 3526
Center 6 • Mat A

Student 2

EMC 3526
Center 6 • Mat A

Student 2

EMC 3526
Center 6 • Mat A

Student 2

EMC 3526
Center 6 • Mat A

Student 2

EMC 3526
Center 6 • Mat A

Student 2

EMC 3526
Center 6 • Mat A

Student 1

EMC 3526
Center 6 • Mat A

Student 1

EMC 3526
Center 6 • Mat A

Student 2

EMC 3526
Center 6 • Mat A

Student 1

EMC 3526
Center 6 • Mat A

Student 1

EMC 3526
Center 6 • Mat A

Student 1

EMC 3526
Center 6 • Mat A

Student 1

EMC 3526
Center 6 • Mat A

Student 1

EMC 3526
Center 6 • Mat A

Student 4

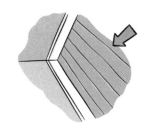

Student 3

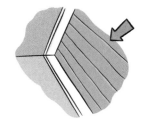

Student 4
EMC 3526
Center 6 • Mat A

Student 4
EMC 3526
Center 6 • Mat A

Student 4
EMC 3526
Center 6 • Mat A

Student 4
EMC 3526
Center 6 • Mat A

Student 4
EMC 3526
Center 6 • Mat A

Student 4
EMC 3526
Center 6 • Mat A

Student 4
EMC 3526
Center 6 • Mat A

Student 4
EMC 3526
Center 6 • Mat A

Student 4
EMC 3526
Center 6 • Mat A

Student 3
EMC 3526
Center 6 • Mat A

Student 3
EMC 3526
Center 6 • Mat A

Student 3
EMC 3526
Center 6 • Mat A

Student 3
EMC 3526
Center 6 • Mat A

Student 3
EMC 3526
Center 6 • Mat A

Student 3
EMC 3526
Center 6 • Mat A

Student 3
EMC 3526
Center 6 • Mat A

Student 3
EMC 3526
Center 6 • Mat A

Student 3
EMC 3526
Center 6 • Mat A

Student 6

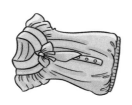

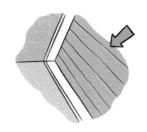

Student 5

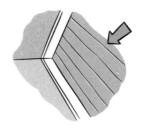

Student 6

EMC 3526
Center 6 • Mat A

Student 6

EMC 3526
Center 6 • Mat A

Student 6

EMC 3526
Center 6 • Mat A

Student 5

EMC 3526
Center 6 • Mat A

Student 6

EMC 3526
Center 6 • Mat A

Student 6

EMC 3526
Center 6 • Mat A

Student 5

EMC 3526
Center 6 • Mat A

Student 5

EMC 3526
Center 6 • Mat A

Student 6

EMC 3526
Center 6 • Mat A

Student 5

EMC 3526
Center 6 • Mat A

Student 5

EMC 3526
Center 6 • Mat A

Student 5

EMC 3526
Center 6 • Mat A

Student 2

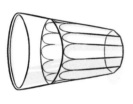
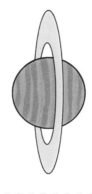
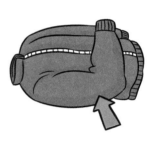

Student 1

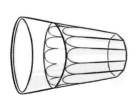
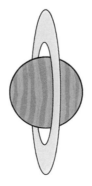

Student 2

Student 2

Student 2

Student 2

Student 2

Student 2

Student 1

Student 1

Student 1

Student 1

Student 1

Student 1

Student 4

Student 3

Student 4

EMC 3526 • Center 6 • Mat B

Student 4

EMC 3526 • Center 6 • Mat B

Student 4

EMC 3526 • Center 6 • Mat B

Student 4

EMC 3526 • Center 6 • Mat B

Student 4

EMC 3526 • Center 6 • Mat B

Student 3

EMC 3526 • Center 6 • Mat B

Student 3

EMC 3526 • Center 6 • Mat B

Student 3

EMC 3526 • Center 6 • Mat B

Student 3

EMC 3526 • Center 6 • Mat B

Student 3

EMC 3526 • Center 6 • Mat B

Student 3

EMC 3526 • Center 6 • Mat B

Student 6

Student 5

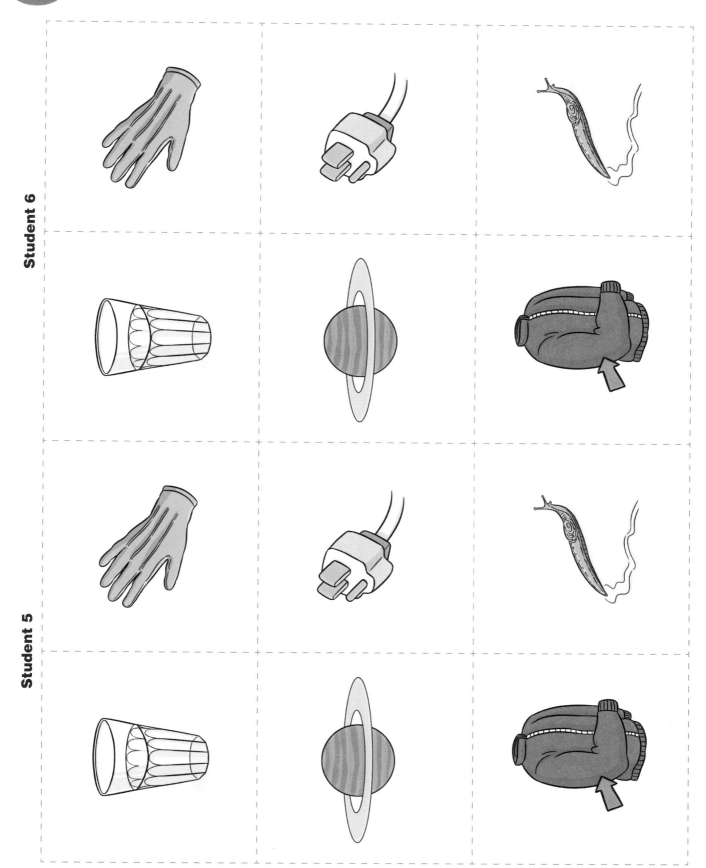

Student 6

EMC 3526 • Center 6 • Mat B

Student 6

EMC 3526 • Center 6 • Mat B

Student 6

EMC 3526 • Center 6 • Mat B

Student 6

EMC 3526 • Center 6 • Mat B

Student 6

EMC 3526 • Center 6 • Mat B

Student 5

EMC 3526 • Center 6 • Mat B

Student 5

EMC 3526 • Center 6 • Mat B

Student 5

EMC 3526 • Center 6 • Mat B

Student 5

EMC 3526 • Center 6 • Mat B

Practice It!

Say the word that names the picture.
Listen to the beginning sounds.
Write the two missing letters on the lines.

bl   cl   fl   gl   pl   sl

1.

—— —— u m

2.

—— —— u g

3.

—— —— o c k

4.

—— —— o t

5.

—— —— a m e

6.

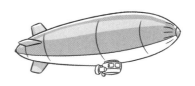

—— —— i m p

7.

—— —— a n t

8.

—— —— y

9.

—— —— o b e

Read It!

Write the word on the line that best completes the sentence.

1. Stars _____ in the sky.
blow   flow   glow

2. My dog can do a _____ in the air.
clip   flip   slip

3. I live one _____ from the mall.
block   clock   flock

4. This baby is thin, but that one is _____.
clump   plump   slump

5. The _____ is dry, so it will not stick.
blue   clue   glue

6. Glen could hear the door _____ shut.
click   flick   slick

7. The baby robin must _____ its wings to fly.
clap   flap   slap

8. Put your money in the _____ to buy some gum.
blot   plot   slot

Initial s Blends

For the Teacher

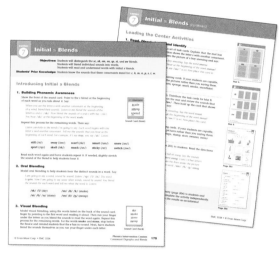

Lesson Plan

Sound Cards

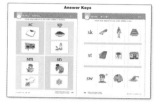

Answer Keys

For the Student

front (Mat A)

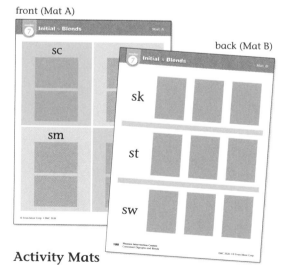

back (Mat B)

Activity Mats

Task Cards

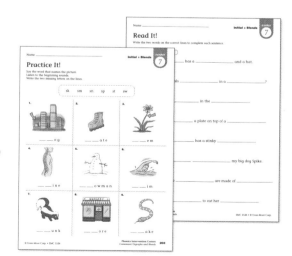

Practice and Assessment Activities

Initial s Blends

Objectives: Students will distinguish the *sc*, *sk*, *sm*, *sn*, *sp*, *st*, and *sw* blends.
Students will blend individual sounds into words.
Students will read and understand words with initial *s* blends.

Students' Prior Knowledge: Students know the sounds that these consonants stand for: *c*, *k*, *m*, *n*, *p*, *s*, *t*, *w*.

Introducing Initial s Blends

1. Building Phonemic Awareness

Show the front of the sound card. Point to the *s* blend at the beginning of each word as you talk about it. Say:

When you see the letter s with another consonant at the beginning of a word, blend their sounds. Listen to me blend the sounds of the letters s and c: /sk/. Now blend the sounds of s and c with me. (/sk/) You hear /sk/ at the beginning of the word scale.

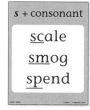

Sound Card (front)

Repeat this process for the remaining words. Then say:

Listen carefully to the words I'm going to say. Each word begins with the letter s and another consonant. Tell me the sounds that you hear at the beginning of each word. For example, if I say step, you say /st/. Listen:

still (/st/)	**sway** (/sw/)	**scarf** (/sk/)	**smart** (/sm/)	**snore** (/sn/)
sport (/sp/)	**skull** (/sk/)	**snack** (/sn/)	**sticky** (/st/)	**switch** (/sw/)

Read each word again and have students repeat it. If needed, slightly stretch the sound of the blend to help students hear it.

2. Oral Blending

Model oral blending to help students hear the distinct sounds in a word. Say:

I am going to say a word, sound by sound. Listen: /sp/ /ĭ/ /n/. The word is spin. Now I am going to say some other words, sound by sound. You blend the sounds for each word and tell me what the word is. Listen:

/sk/ /ī/ (sky)	/sn/ /ā/ /k/ (snake)
/st/ /ō/ /n/ (stone)	/sw/ /ē/ /p/ (sweep)

3. Visual Blending

Model visual blending, using the words listed on the back of the sound card. Begin by pointing to the first word and reading it aloud. Then run your finger under the letters as you blend the sounds to read the word again. Repeat this process for the remaining words. For the words **snake** and **stone**, stop before the final *e* and remind students that the *e* has no sound. Next, have students blend the sounds themselves as you run your finger under each letter.

Sound Card (back)

Leading the Center Activities

1. Read, Discriminate, and Identify ....

Give each student Mat A and a set of task cards. Explain that the mat has four sections and that each section shows the letter *s* with another consonant. Then hold up the card that shows the picture of a boy sneezing and say:

> *This card shows a picture of a boy sneezing. Say the word* **sneeze**. (sneeze) *What sounds do you hear at the beginning of the word* **sneeze**? (/sn/) *Which letters on the mat say* /**sn**/? (s-n) *Now place this card in the* **s-n** *section of the mat.*

Repeat this process with the remaining cards. If your students are capable, have them tell you the names of the pictures rather than you saying them. (scale, score or scoreboard, spaghetti, sponge, smell, smoke, snowflake)

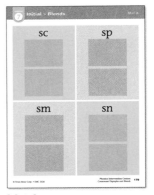

Mat A

2. Read and Understand ....

Have students turn over their mats. Distribute the task cards for Mat B. Point out the three rows of blends on the mat and review the sounds that each blend stands for: /**sk**/, /**st**/, /**sw**/. Then hold up the card that shows the picture of a man sweating and say:

> *This card shows a picture of a man sweating. Say the word* **sweat**. (sweat) *What sounds do you hear at the beginning of the word* **sweat**? (/sw/) *Which letters on the mat say* /**sw**/? (s-w) *Now place this card in the row for* **s-w**.

Repeat this process with the remaining cards. If your students are capable, have them tell you the names of the pictures rather than you saying them. (skateboard, skeleton, skirt, stairs or steps, stamp, store, sweater, swim)

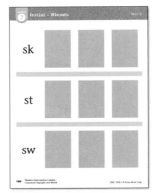

Mat B

3. Practice the Skill ....

Distribute the Practice It! activity (page 203) to students. Read the directions aloud. Then say:

> *Look at the first picture. It shows a city full of smog. Say the sounds that you hear at the beginning of the word* **smog**. (/sm/) *What letters say* /**sm**/? (s-m) *Write the letters* **s-m** *on the lines under the picture. Now let's blend the sounds and read the word:* /sm/ /ŏ/ /g/ smog.

Repeat this process to complete the page.

Page 203

Apply and Assess

After the lesson, distribute the Read It! activity (page 204) to students and read the directions aloud. Have students complete the activity independently. Then listen to them read the sentences. Use the results as an informal assessment of students' skill mastery.

Page 204

s + consonant

scale

smog

spend

Center 7 • Sound Card

Answer Keys

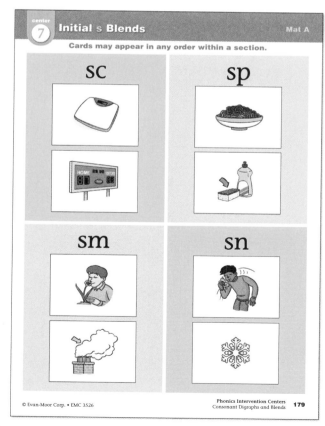

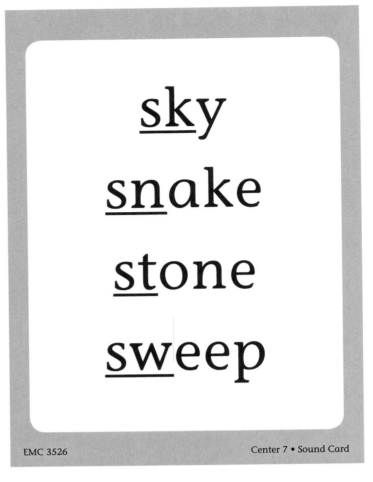

sky

<u>sn</u>ake

<u>st</u>one

<u>sw</u>eep

EMC 3526   Center 7 • Sound Card

Answer Keys

Name _____

Initial s Blends   center **7**

Practice It!

Say the word that names the picture.
Listen to the beginning sounds.
Write the two missing letters on the lines.

| sk | sm | sn | sp | st | sw |

1. <u>sm</u>og
2. <u>sk</u>ate
3. <u>st</u>em
4. <u>sp</u>ine
5. <u>sn</u>owman
6. <u>sw</u>im
7. <u>sk</u>unk
8. <u>st</u>ore
9. <u>sn</u>ake

© Evan-Moor Corp. • EMC 3526   Phonics Intervention Centers
Consonant Digraphs and Blends   **203**

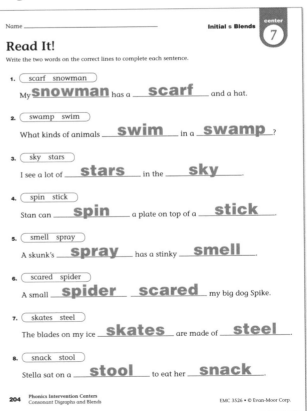

Name _____

Initial s Blends   center **7**

Read It!

Write the two words on the correct lines to complete each sentence.

1. (scarf snowman)
   My **snowman** has a **scarf** and a hat.

2. (swamp swim)
   What kinds of animals **swim** in a **swamp**?

3. (sky stars)
   I see a lot of **stars** in the **sky**.

4. (spin stick)
   Stan can **spin** a plate on top of a **stick**.

5. (smell spray)
   A skunk's **spray** has a stinky **smell**.

6. (scared spider)
   A small **spider** **scared** my big dog Spike.

7. (skates steel)
   The blades on my ice **skates** are made of **steel**.

8. (snack stool)
   Stella sat on a **stool** to eat her **snack**.

204   Phonics Intervention Centers
Consonant Digraphs and Blends   EMC 3526 • © Evan-Moor Corp.

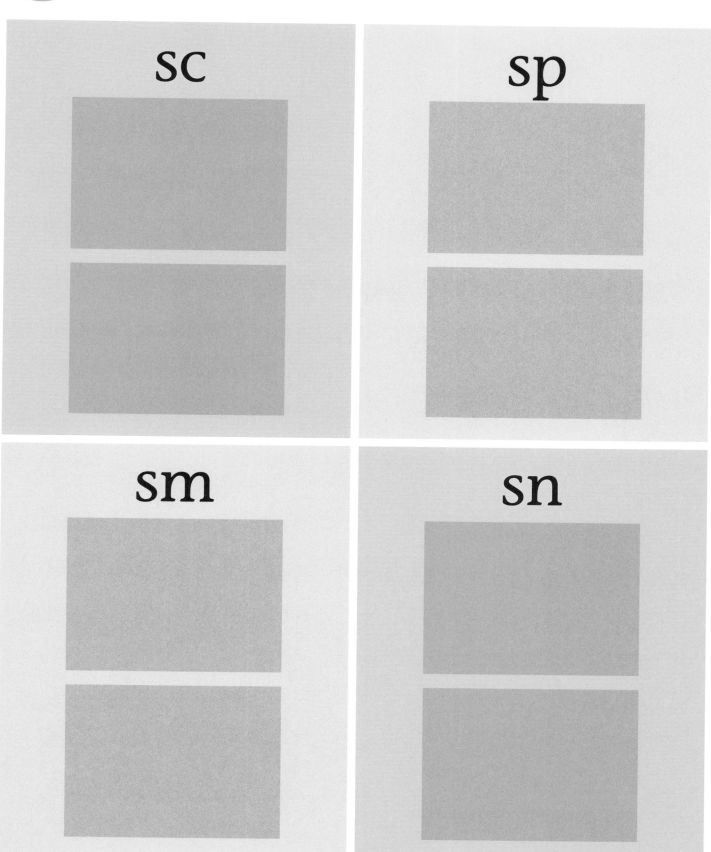

sc

sp

sm

sn

sk

st

sw

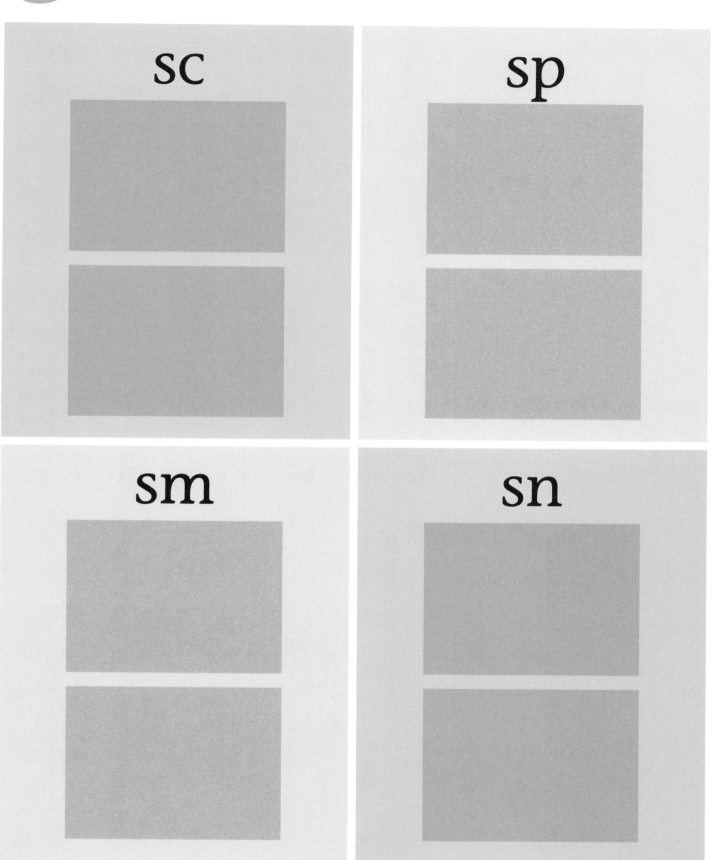

sc

sp

sm

sn

sk

st

sw

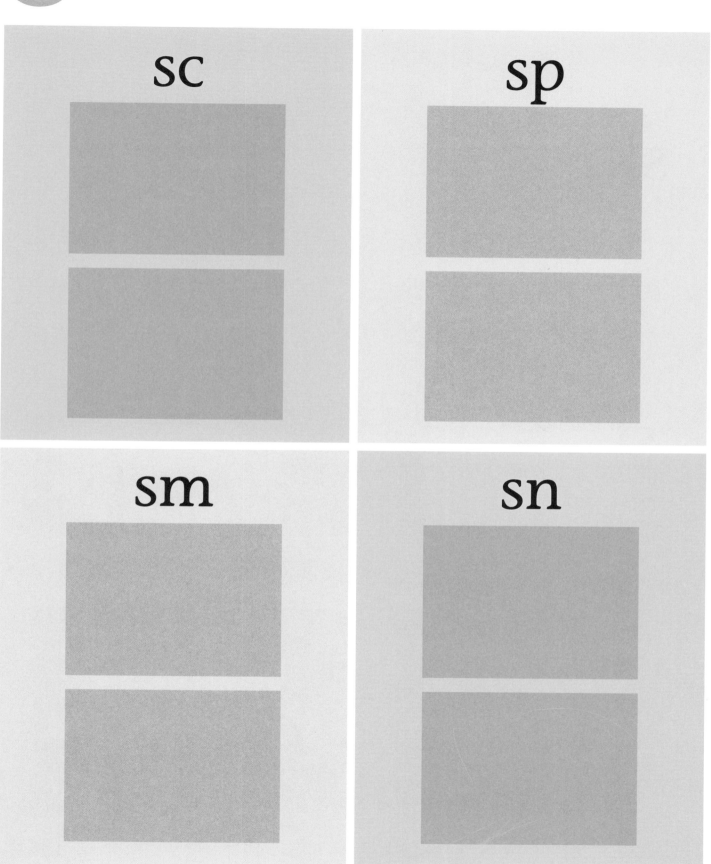

sc

sp

sm

sn

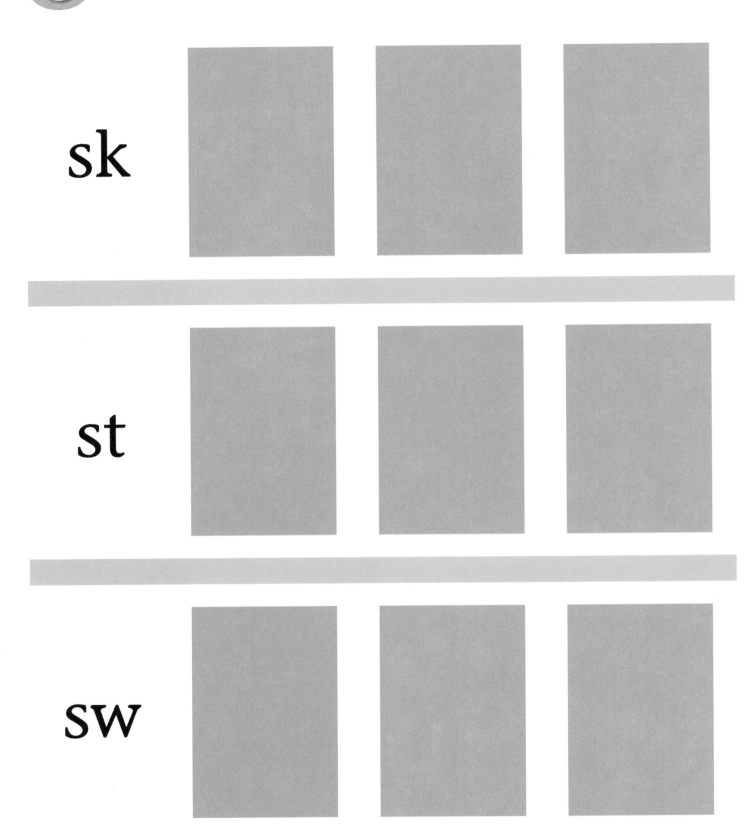

sk

st

sw

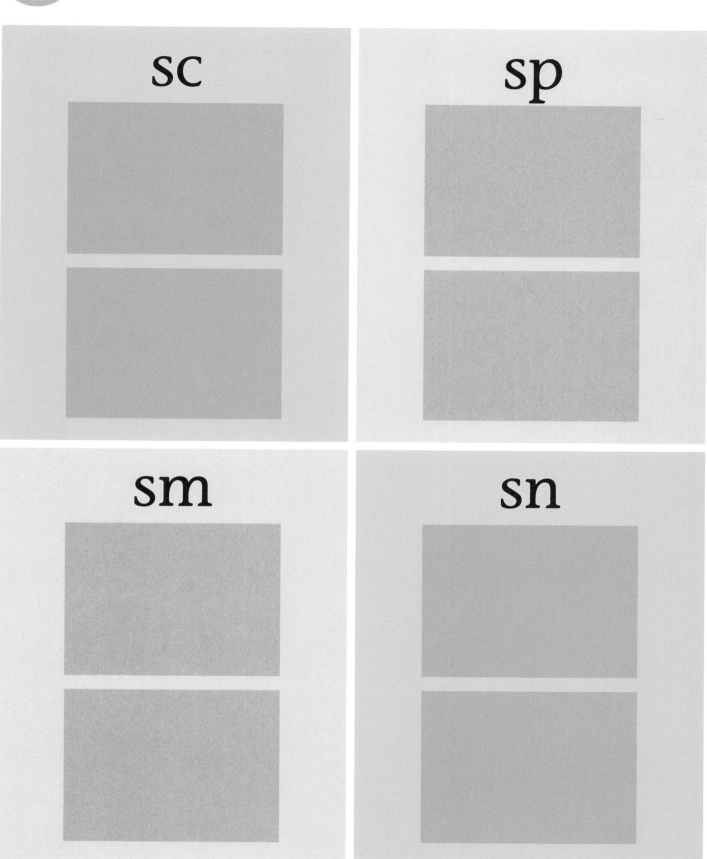

sc

sp

sm

sn

sk

st

sw

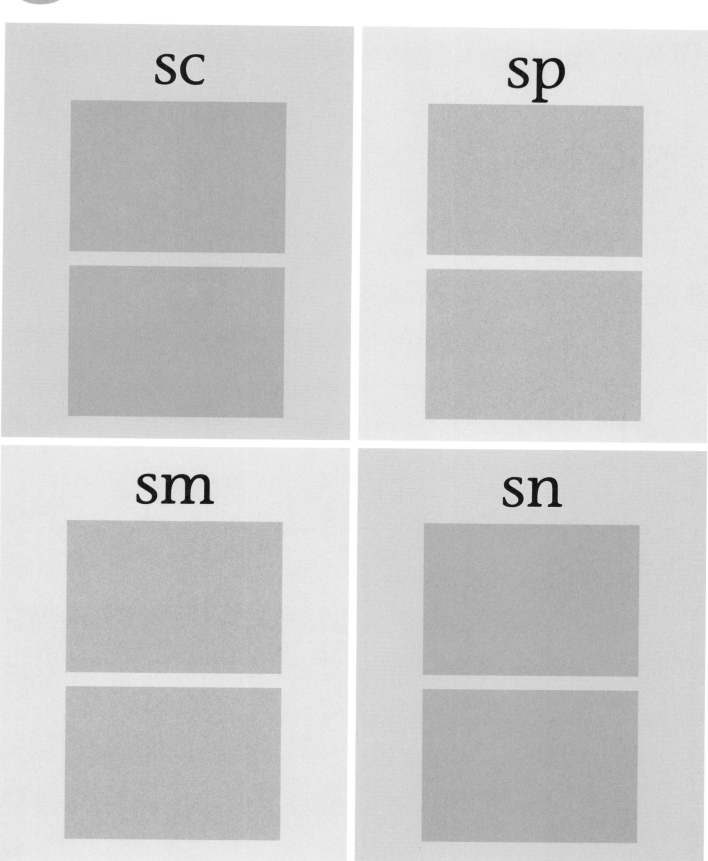

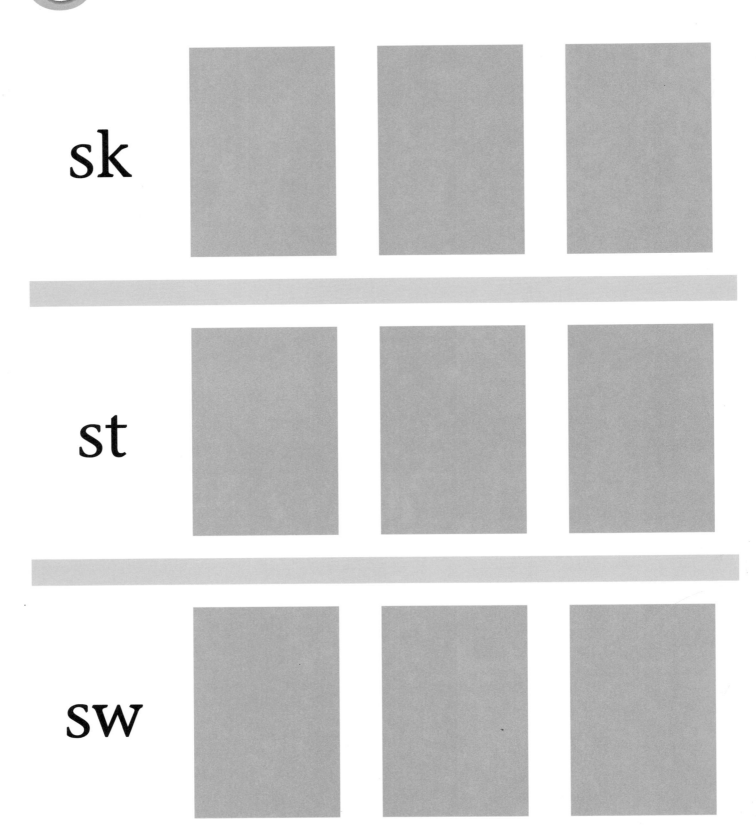

sk

st

sw

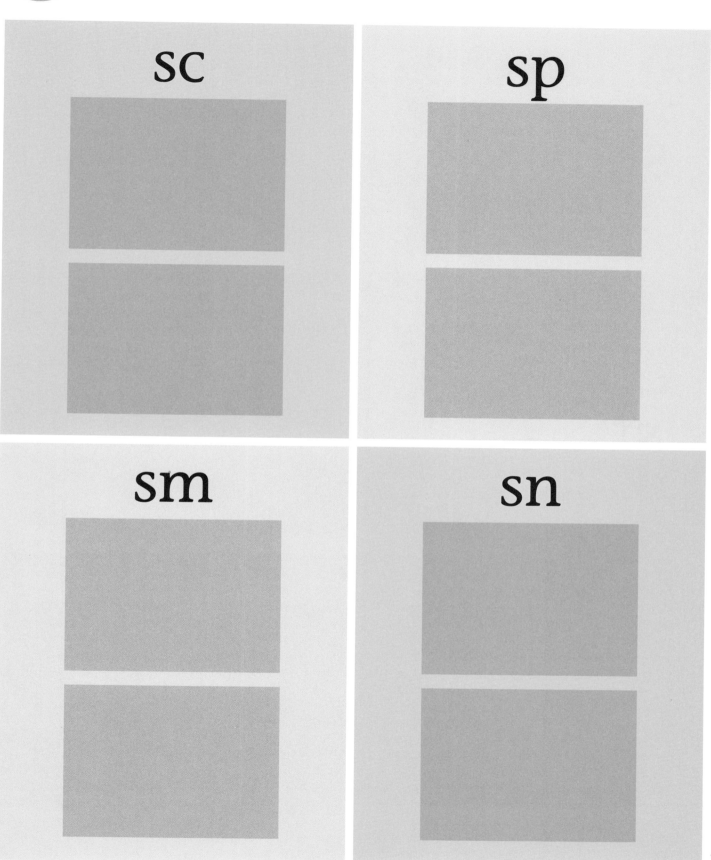

sc

sp

sm

sn

sk

st

sw

Student 2

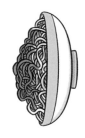

Student 1

Student 2

EMC 3526 • Center 7 • Mat A

Student 2

EMC 3526 • Center 7 • Mat A

Student 2

EMC 3526 • Center 7 • Mat A

Student 2

EMC 3526 • Center 7 • Mat A

Student 2

EMC 3526 • Center 7 • Mat A

Student 2

EMC 3526 • Center 7 • Mat A

Student 2

EMC 3526 • Center 7 • Mat A

Student 1

EMC 3526 • Center 7 • Mat A

Student 1

EMC 3526 • Center 7 • Mat A

Student 1

EMC 3526 • Center 7 • Mat A

Student 1

EMC 3526 • Center 7 • Mat A

Student 1

EMC 3526 • Center 7 • Mat A

Student 1

EMC 3526 • Center 7 • Mat A

Student 1

EMC 3526 • Center 7 • Mat A

Student 4

Student 3

Student 4

EMC 3526 • Center 7 • Mat A

Student 4

EMC 3526 • Center 7 • Mat A

Student 4

EMC 3526 • Center 7 • Mat A

Student 4

EMC 3526 • Center 7 • Mat A

Student 3

EMC 3526 • Center 7 • Mat A

Student 4

EMC 3526 • Center 7 • Mat A

Student 4

EMC 3526 • Center 7 • Mat A

Student 3

EMC 3526 • Center 7 • Mat A

Student 3

EMC 3526 • Center 7 • Mat A

Student 3

EMC 3526 • Center 7 • Mat A

Student 3

EMC 3526 • Center 7 • Mat A

Student 3

EMC 3526 • Center 7 • Mat A

Student 3

EMC 3526 • Center 7 • Mat A

Student 3

EMC 3526 • Center 7 • Mat A

Task Cards

Student 6

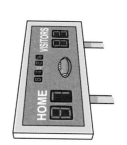   

 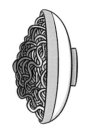  

Student 5

© Evan-Moor Corp. • EMC 3526

Phonics Intervention Centers
Consonant Digraphs and Blends **195**

Student 6

EMC 3526 • Center 7 • Mat A

Student 6

EMC 3526 • Center 7 • Mat A

Student 6

EMC 3526 • Center 7 • Mat A

Student 6

EMC 3526 • Center 7 • Mat A

Student 6

EMC 3526 • Center 7 • Mat A

Student 6

EMC 3526 • Center 7 • Mat A

Student 5

EMC 3526 • Center 7 • Mat A

Student 5

EMC 3526 • Center 7 • Mat A

Student 5

EMC 3526 • Center 7 • Mat A

Student 5

EMC 3526 • Center 7 • Mat A

Student 5

EMC 3526 • Center 7 • Mat A

Student 5

EMC 3526 • Center 7 • Mat A

Student 2

Student 1

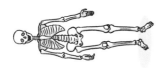

Student 2

EMC 3526
Center 7 • Mat B

Student 2

EMC 3526
Center 7 • Mat B

Student 2

EMC 3526
Center 7 • Mat B

Student 2

EMC 3526
Center 7 • Mat B

Student 2

EMC 3526
Center 7 • Mat B

Student 2

EMC 3526
Center 7 • Mat B

Student 1

EMC 3526
Center 7 • Mat B

Student 2

EMC 3526
Center 7 • Mat B

Student 1

EMC 3526
Center 7 • Mat B

Student 1

EMC 3526
Center 7 • Mat B

Student 2

EMC 3526
Center 7 • Mat B

Student 1

EMC 3526
Center 7 • Mat B

Student 1

EMC 3526
Center 7 • Mat B

Student 1

EMC 3526
Center 7 • Mat B

Student 1

EMC 3526
Center 7 • Mat B

Phonics Intervention Centers
Consonant Digraphs and Blends

EMC 3526 • © Evan-Moor Corp.

Student 4

Student 3

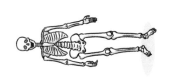  

Student 4

EMC 3526
Center 7 • Mat B

Student 4

EMC 3526
Center 7 • Mat B

Student 4

EMC 3526
Center 7 • Mat B

Student 4

EMC 3526
Center 7 • Mat B

Student 4

EMC 3526
Center 7 • Mat B

Student 4

EMC 3526
Center 7 • Mat B

Student 4

EMC 3526
Center 7 • Mat B

Student 3

EMC 3526
Center 7 • Mat B

Student 4

EMC 3526
Center 7 • Mat B

Student 3

EMC 3526
Center 7 • Mat B

Student 3

EMC 3526
Center 7 • Mat B

Student 3

EMC 3526
Center 7 • Mat B

Student 3

EMC 3526
Center 7 • Mat B

Student 3

EMC 3526
Center 7 • Mat B

Student 3

EMC 3526
Center 7 • Mat B

Student 3

EMC 3526
Center 7 • Mat B

Student 6

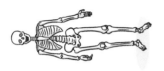

Student 5

Student 6

EMC 3526
Center 7 • Mat B

Student 6

EMC 3526
Center 7 • Mat B

Student 6

EMC 3526
Center 7 • Mat B

Student 6

EMC 3526
Center 7 • Mat B

Student 6

EMC 3526
Center 7 • Mat B

Student 6

EMC 3526
Center 7 • Mat B

Student 6

EMC 3526
Center 7 • Mat B

Student 5

EMC 3526
Center 7 • Mat B

Student 5

EMC 3526
Center 7 • Mat B

Student 5

EMC 3526
Center 7 • Mat B

Student 5

EMC 3526
Center 7 • Mat B

Student 5

EMC 3526
Center 7 • Mat B

Student 5

EMC 3526
Center 7 • Mat B

Student 5

EMC 3526
Center 7 • Mat B

Practice It!

Say the word that names the picture.
Listen to the beginning sounds.
Write the two missing letters on the lines.

| sk | sm | sn | sp | st | sw |

1.

____ ____ o g

2.

____ ____ a t e

3.

____ ____ e m

4.

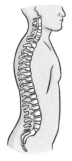

____ ____ i n e

5.

____ ____ o w m a n

6.

____ ____ i m

7.

____ ____ u n k

8.

____ ____ o r e

9.

____ ____ a k e

Read It!

Write the two words on the correct lines to complete each sentence.

1. (scarf   snowman)

My _____ has a _____ and a hat.

2. (swamp   swim)

What kinds of animals _____ in a _____?

3. (sky   stars)

I see a lot of _____ in the _____.

4. (spin   stick)

Stan can _____ a plate on top of a _____.

5. (smell   spray)

A skunk's _____ has a stinky _____.

6. (scared   spider)

A small _____ _____ my big dog Spike.

7. (skates   steel)

The blades on my ice _____ are made of _____.

8. (snack   stool)

Stella sat on a _____ to eat her _____.

Consonant Blends Review

For the Teacher

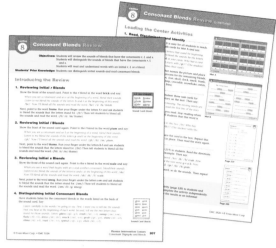

Lesson Plan

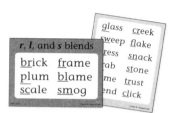

Sound Cards

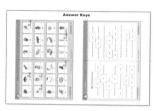

Answer Keys

For the Student

> To make Mat A, place pages 212 and 213 side by side and laminate. (Turn over for Mat B.)

front (Mat A)

back (Mat B)

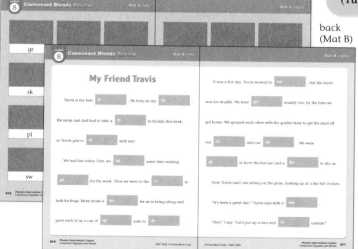

Activity Mats

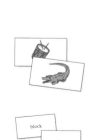

Task Cards

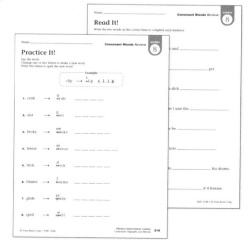

Practice and Assessment Activities

Consonant Blends Review

Objectives: Students will review the sounds of blends that have the consonants *r*, *l*, and *s*.
Students will distinguish the sounds of blends that have the consonants *r*, *l*, and *s*.
Students will read and understand words with an initial *r*, *l*, or *s* blend.

Students' Prior Knowledge: Students can distinguish initial sounds and read consonant blends.

Introducing the Review

1. Reviewing Initial *r* Blends

Show the front of the sound card. Point to the *r* blend in the word **brick** and say:

When you see a consonant and an r at the beginning of a word, blend their sounds.
Listen to me blend the sounds of the letters b and r at the beginning of this word:
/br/. Now I'll blend all the sounds and read the word: /br/ /ĭ/ /k/ brick.

Next, point to the word **frame**. Run your finger under the letters *f-r* and ask students to blend the sounds that the letters stand for. (/fr/) Then tell students to blend all the sounds and read the word. (/fr/ /ā/ /m/ frame)

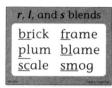

r, l, and *s* blends

brick	frame
plum	blame
scale	smog

Sound Card (front)

2. Reviewing Initial *l* Blends

Show the front of the sound card again. Point to the *l* blend in the word **plum** and say:

When you see a consonant and an l at the beginning of a word, blend their sounds.
Listen to me blend the sounds of the letters p and l at the beginning of this word:
/pl/. Now I'll blend all the sounds and read the word: /pl/ /ŭ/ /m/ plum.

Next, point to the word **blame**. Run your finger under the letters *b-l* and ask students to blend the sounds that the letters stand for. (/bl/) Then tell students to blend all the sounds and read the word. (/bl/ /ā/ /m/ blame)

3. Reviewing Initial *s* Blends

Show the front of the sound card again. Point to the *s* blend in the word **scale** and say:

When you see a word that begins with an s and another consonant, blend their sounds.
Listen to me blend the sounds of the letters s and c at the beginning of this word: /sk/.
Now I'll blend all the sounds and read the word: /sk/ /ā/ /l/ scale.

Next, point to the word **smog**. Run your finger under the letters *s-m* and ask students to blend the sounds that the letters stand for. (/sm/) Then tell students to blend all the sounds and read the word. (/sm/ /ŏ/ /g/ smog)

4. Distinguishing Initial Consonant Blends

Have students listen for the consonant blends in the words listed on the back of the sound card. Say:

*Listen carefully to the words I'm going to say. First, I want you to tell me the sounds that you hear at the beginning of each word. Second, tell me the two letters that stand for those sounds. Listen: **glass** (/gl/, g-l), **creek** (/kr/, c-r), **sweep** (/sw/, s-w), **flake** (/fl/, f-l), **dress** (/dr/, d-r), **snack** (/sn/, s-n), **grab** (/gr/, g-r), **stone** (/st/, s-t), **slime** (/sl/, s-l), **trust** (/tr/, t-r), **spend** (/sp/, s-p), **click** (/kl/, c-l).*

glass	creek
sweep	flake
dress	snack
grab	stone
slime	trust
spend	click

Sound Card (back)

Leading the Center Activities

1. Read, Discriminate, and Identify ·····················

Place Mat A on a table where it is easy for all students to reach. Then give each student four task cards for Mat A and say:

Each box on this mat has two letters that stand for beginning sounds you have learned. Let's blend the sounds for the letters in the first box: /gr/. Now look at your cards. Who has a card with the picture of a word that starts with /gr/? (The student with the picture of grapes shows that card.)

Have the student say the word that names the picture and place the card in the box. Repeat this process for the remaining blends. (spaghetti, flashlight, stove, drum, clue; skull, clock, smell, trunk, blimp, grill; plant, scale, bread, sleep, crocodile, snowflake; swim, pretzel, skate, glass, spine, french fries)

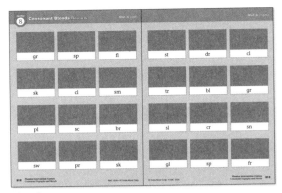

Mat A

2. Read and Understand ·····························

Turn over the mat and give each student three task cards for Mat B. Read aloud the title of the story on the mat. Then say:

Some of the words in this story are missing. The missing words are on your cards. Listen carefully as I read the first line of the story.

Run your finger under the words as you read. Stop reading when you get to the first green box and tell students that this word is missing. Then say:

Let's blend the sounds for the letters in this box: /fr/. Who has a card with a word that starts with /fr/? (The student with the word *friend* shows that card.)

Have the student say the word and place the card in the box. Repeat this process until all the missing words are in place. Then read the story again.

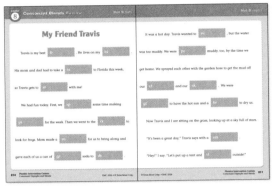

Mat B

3. Practice the Skill ·································

Distribute the Practice It! activity (page 219) to students. Read the directions aloud and guide students through the example. Then say:

*Let's blend the sounds to read the first word: /kr/ /ă/ /b/ crab. Now let's change the letter **c** to a **g** and write the new word: **g-r-a-b**. Now blend the sounds and read the new word: /gr/ /ă/ /b/ grab.*

Tell students that as letters change in a word, so do the sounds. Then repeat this process with the remaining words.

Page 219

Apply and Assess

After the lesson, distribute the Read It! activity (page 220) to students and read the directions aloud. Have students complete the activity independently. Then listen to them read the sentences. Use the results as an informal assessment of students' skill mastery.

Page 220

r, l, and *s* blends

brick frame

plum blame

scale smog

Center 8 • Sound Card

EMC 3526

Answer Keys

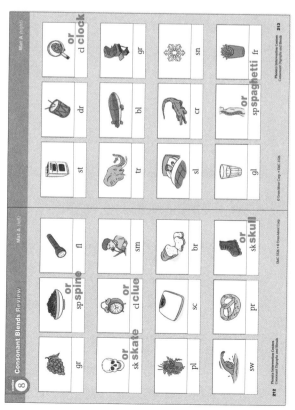

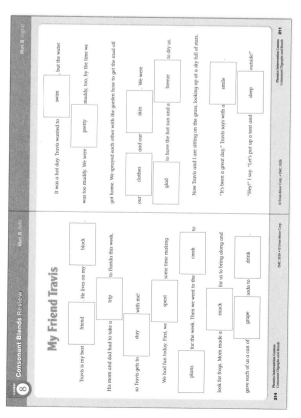

glass creek

sweep flake

dress snack

grab stone

slime trust

spend click

EMC 3526 Center 8 • Sound Card

Answer Keys

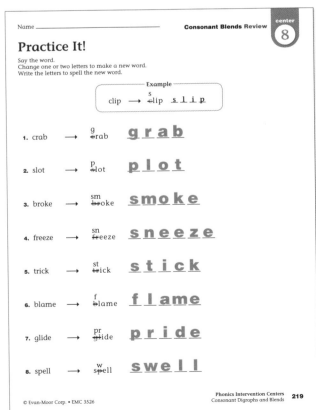

Name _____ Consonant Blends Review center 8

Practice It!

Say the word.
Change one or two letters to make a new word.
Write the letters to spell the new word.

Example

clip → ~~c~~lip s l i p (s above)

1. crab → ~~c~~rab (g above) **g r a b**

2. slot → ~~s~~lot (p above) **p l o t**

3. broke → ~~br~~oke (sm above) **s m o k e**

4. freeze → ~~fr~~eeze (sn above) **s n e e z e**

5. trick → ~~tr~~ick (st above) **s t i c k**

6. blame → ~~bl~~ame (f above) **f l a m e**

7. glide → ~~gl~~ide (pr above) **p r i d e**

8. spell → ~~sp~~ell (w above) **s w e l l**

© Evan-Moor Corp. • EMC 3526 Phonics Intervention Centers Consonant Digraphs and Blends **219**

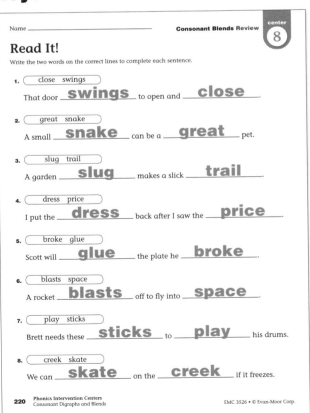

Name _____ Consonant Blends Review center 8

Read It!

Write the two words on the correct lines to complete each sentence.

1. close swings
   That door **swings** to open and **close** .

2. great snake
   A small **snake** can be a **great** pet.

3. slug trail
   A garden **slug** makes a slick **trail** .

4. dress price
   I put the **dress** back after I saw the **price** .

5. broke glue
   Scott will **glue** the plate he **broke** .

6. blasts space
   A rocket **blasts** off to fly into **space** .

7. play sticks
   Brett needs these **sticks** to **play** his drums.

8. creek skate
   We can **skate** on the **creek** if it freezes.

220 Phonics Intervention Centers Consonant Digraphs and Blends EMC 3526 • © Evan-Moor Corp.

It was a hot day. Travis wanted to [sw] , but the water

was too muddy. We were [pr] muddy, too, by the time we

got home. We sprayed each other with the garden hose to get the mud off

our [cl] and our [sk] . We were

[gl] to have the hot sun and a [br] to dry us.

Now Travis and I are sitting on the grass, looking up at a sky full of stars.

"It's been a great day," Travis says with a [sm] .

"Hey!" I say. "Let's put up a tent and [sl] outside!"

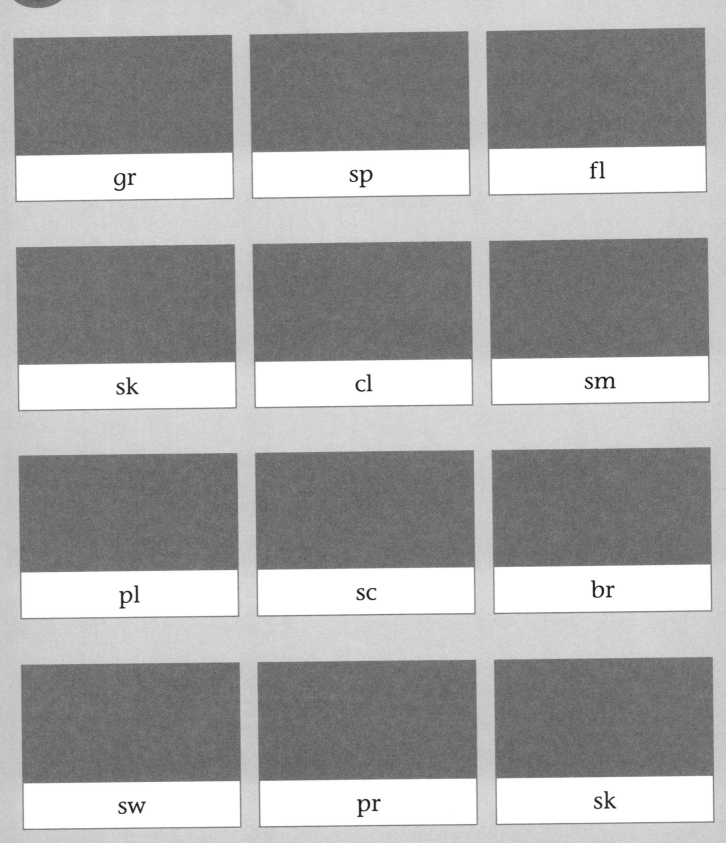

gr

sp

fl

sk

cl

sm

pl

sc

br

sw

pr

sk

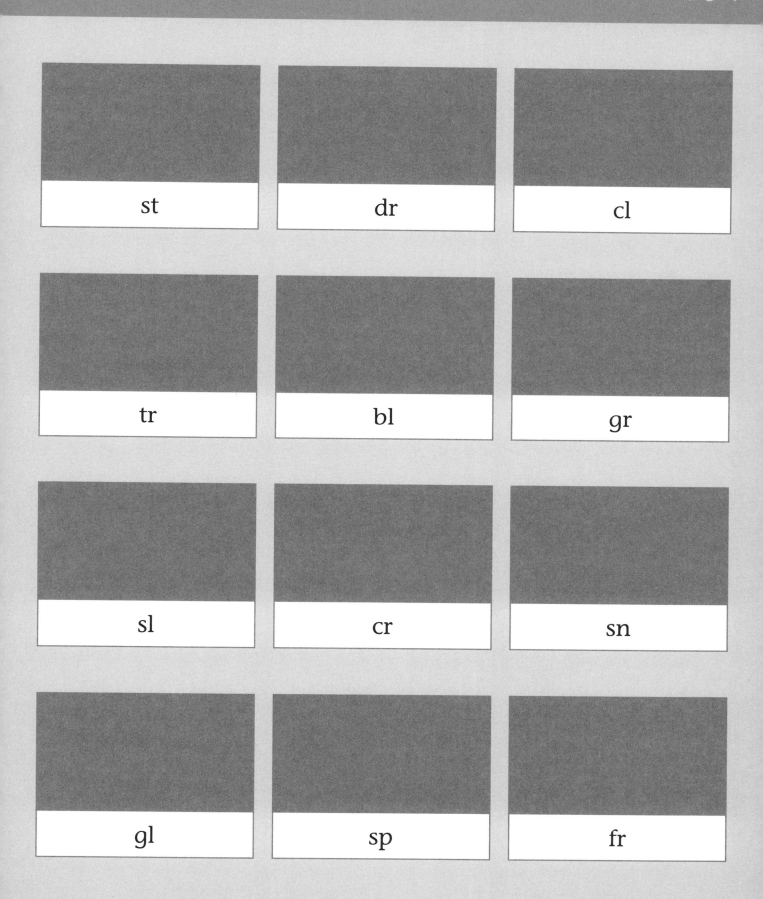

st

dr

cl

tr

bl

gr

sl

cr

sn

gl

sp

fr

My Friend Travis

Travis is my best fr   . He lives on my bl   .

His mom and dad had to take a tr   to Florida this week,

so Travis gets to st   with me!

We had fun today. First, we sp   some time making

pl   for the week. Then we went to the cr   to

look for frogs. Mom made a sn   for us to bring along and

gave each of us a can of gr   soda to dr   .

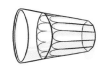

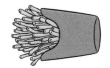

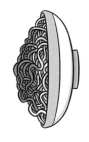

Phonics Intervention Centers
Consonant Digraphs and Blends 215

EMC 3526 • Center 8 • Mat A

EMC 3526 • Center 8 • Mat A

EMC 3526 • Center 8 • Mat A

EMC 3526 • Center 8 • Mat A

EMC 3526 • Center 8 • Mat A

EMC 3526 • Center 8 • Mat A

EMC 3526 • Center 8 • Mat A

EMC 3526 • Center 8 • Mat A

EMC 3526 • Center 8 • Mat A

EMC 3526 • Center 8 • Mat A

EMC 3526 • Center 8 • Mat A

EMC 3526 • Center 8 • Mat A

EMC 3526 • Center 8 • Mat A

EMC 3526 • Center 8 • Mat A

EMC 3526 • Center 8 • Mat A

EMC 3526 • Center 8 • Mat A

EMC 3526 • Center 8 • Mat A

EMC 3526 • Center 8 • Mat A

friend	block	trip
stay	spent	plans
creek	snack	grape
drink	swim	pretty
clothes	skin	glad
breeze	smile	sleep

EMC 3526
Center 8 • Mat B

EMC 3526
Center 8 • Mat B

EMC 3526
Center 8 • Mat B

EMC 3526
Center 8 • Mat B

EMC 3526
Center 8 • Mat B

EMC 3526
Center 8 • Mat B

EMC 3526
Center 8 • Mat B

EMC 3526
Center 8 • Mat B

EMC 3526
Center 8 • Mat B

EMC 3526
Center 8 • Mat B

EMC 3526
Center 8 • Mat B

EMC 3526
Center 8 • Mat B

EMC 3526
Center 8 • Mat B

EMC 3526
Center 8 • Mat B

EMC 3526
Center 8 • Mat B

EMC 3526
Center 8 • Mat B

EMC 3526
Center 8 • Mat B

EMC 3526
Center 8 • Mat B

Practice It!

Say the word.
Change one or two letters to make a new word.
Write the letters to spell the new word.

┌─────────────── Example ───────────────┐

clip ⟶ s̶clip   **s l i p**

└──┘

1. crab ⟶ g̶crab   __ __ __ __

2. slot ⟶ p̶slot   __ __ __ __

3. broke ⟶ sm̶broke   __ __ __ __ __

4. freeze ⟶ sn̶freeze   __ __ __ __ __ __

5. trick ⟶ st̶trick   __ __ __ __

6. blame ⟶ f̶blame   __ __ __ __ __

7. glide ⟶ pr̶glide   __ __ __ __ __

8. spell ⟶ s̶wpell   __ __ __ __ __

Read It!

Write the two words on the correct lines to complete each sentence.

1. (close   swings)

   That door _____ to open and _____.

2. (great   snake)

   A small _____ can be a _____ pet.

3. (slug   trail)

   A garden _____ makes a slick _____.

4. (dress   price)

   I put the _____ back after I saw the _____.

5. (broke   glue)

   Scott will _____ the plate he _____.

6. (blasts   space)

   A rocket _____ off to fly into _____.

7. (play   sticks)

   Brett needs these _____ to _____ his drums.

8. (creek   skate)

   We can _____ on the _____ if it freezes.

Provide students with important reading and language arts skill practice!

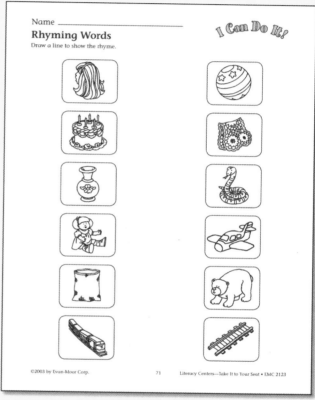

Take It to Your Seat
Literacy Centers

Grade	
PreK–K	EMC 2401
K–1	EMC 2123
1–3	EMC 788
2–3	EMC 2723
3–4	EMC 2124
4–5	EMC 2724
4–6	EMC 2719

Features:

- Provide students with important reading and language arts skill practice that feels more like fun than work!

- Each book comes with up to 18 self-contained centers that students can pick up and take anywhere.

- They're a perfect way to provide students with the extra practice they need to strengthen language skills.

Help your child master math skills!

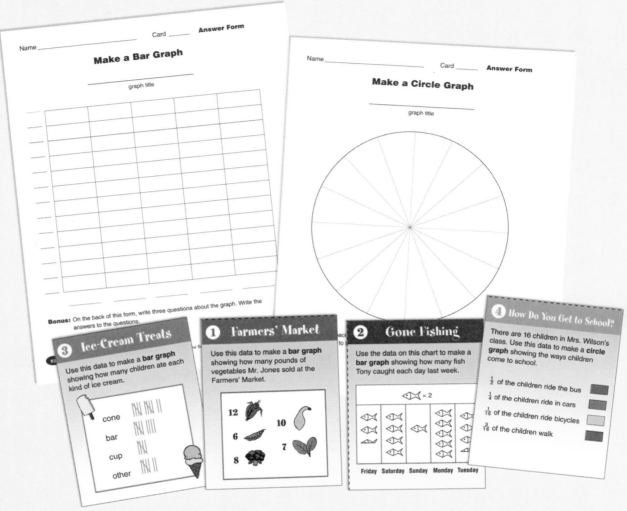

Make a Bar Graph

Name _____
Card _____ Answer Form

_____
graph title

Bonus: On the back of this form, write three questions about the graph. Write the answers to the questions.

Make a Circle Graph

Name _____
Card _____ Answer Form

_____
graph title

③ Ice-Cream Treats

Use this data to make a **bar graph** showing how many children ate each kind of ice cream.

cone
bar
cup
other

① Farmers' Market

Use this data to make a **bar graph** showing how many pounds of vegetables Mr. Jones sold at the Farmers' Market.

12   10
6   7
8

② Gone Fishing

Use the data on this chart to make a **bar graph** showing how many fish Tony caught each day last week.

= 2

Friday   Saturday   Sunday   Monday   Tuesday

④ How Do You Get to School?

There are 16 children in Mrs. Wilson's class. Use this data to make a **circle graph** showing the ways children come to school.

$\frac{1}{2}$ of the children ride the bus

$\frac{1}{4}$ of the children ride in cars

$\frac{1}{16}$ of the children ride bicycles

$\frac{3}{16}$ of the children walk

Features:

- Aligned with NCTM Standards
- Provide fun, hands-on activities
- Help students master numbers and operations, algebra, geometry, measurement, data analysis, and probability
- 192 full-color pages

Take It to Your Seat
Math Centers

Grade	
K–1	EMC 3020
1–3	EMC 3013
2–3	EMC 3021
3–4	EMC 3022
4–6	EMC 3012

Enrich any core writing or language arts program!

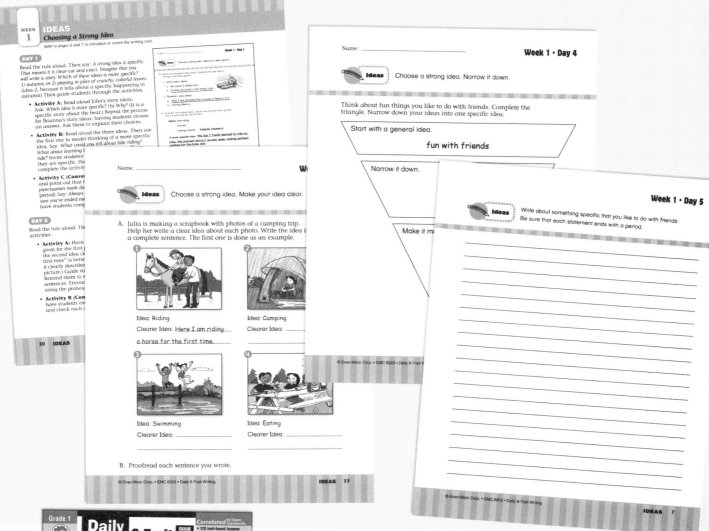

Features:

- 125 scaffolded, trait-based writing lessons

- A trait-based writing rubric

- Teacher pages that include an easy-to-follow teaching path and ideas for modeling and eliciting student responses

- Activities that cover narrative, expository, descriptive, and persuasive writing

Daily 6-Trait Writing

Grade

1	EMC 6021
2	EMC 6022
3	EMC 6023
4	EMC 6024
5	EMC 6025
6+	EMC 6026

Help build your child's language skills!

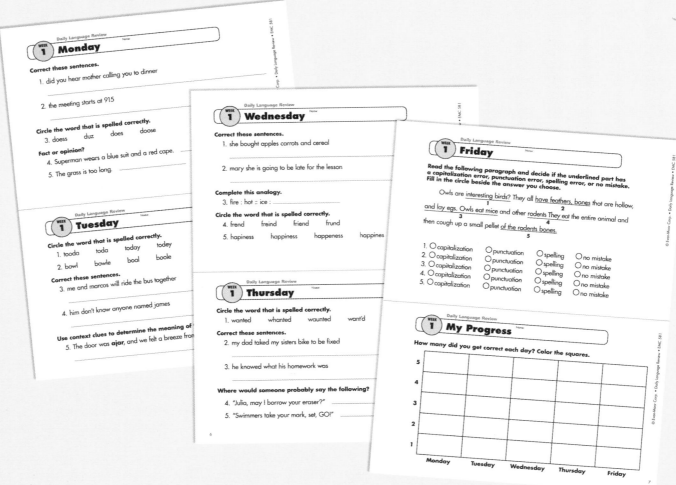

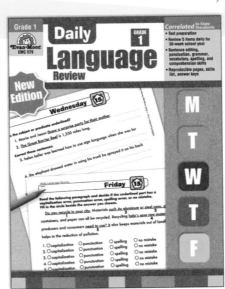

Repeated, focused practice in:

- sentence editing

- corrections in punctuation, capitalization, spelling, grammar, and vocabulary

- additional activities that cover a wide range of language and reading skills

Daily Language Review

Grade

1	EMC 579
2	EMC 580
3	EMC 581
4	EMC 582
5	EMC 583
6	EMC 576
7	EMC 2797
8	EMC 2798